⟨♪ **W9-APG-695**

LIFE!

Also available from Ballantine Books:

THE SAVE-YOUR-LIFE-DIET HIGH-FIBER COOKBOOK by David Reuben, M.D. and Barbara Reuben, M.S.

NOW YOU CAN PUT BACK INTO YOUR DIET THE LIFE-SAVING VITAL INGREDIENT THAT HAS BEEN TAKEN OUT.

This vital ingredient has been enjoyed by humankind throughout all of history—yet within the last century it has been virtually removed from the foods we eat.

In countries where it is still standardly consumed, the most dangerous and common killer diseases of our way of life are virtually unknown.

It can be put into your diet by the expenditure of just 2¢ a day—pennies that can save a fortune in medical bills, not to mention the tragedy of premature and needless death.

In *Everything You Always Wanted to Know About Sex*, David Reuben, M.D., performed a vast and invaluable service of enlightenment in telling us about one of the most important aspects of life. Now he has gone one step further in breaking through the barriers of ignorance and silence to show you how you can dramatically improve and save life itself.

SAVE YOUR

FROM COAST TO COAST, THEY'RE JOINING *THE SAVE YOUR LIFE* CAMPAIGN!

The Save Your Life Diet

High-Fiber Protection from Six of the Most Serious Diseases of Civilization

---

David Reuben, M.D.

BALLANTINE BOOKS • NEW YORK

Library of Congress Catalog Card Number: 75-6653

ISBN 0-345-29678-8

Manufactured in the United States of America

First Ballantine Books Edition: May 1976
Twelfth Printing: December 1982

To my wife, Barbara,
whose love has made everything possible.

An Open Letter to My Fellow Physicians

October 28, 1974

Dear Colleague:

I know that very soon your patients will be bringing you copies of *The Save-Your-Life Diet* and asking you, "Doctor, what do you think of these ideas?" It is of course a sign of the confidence they place in you and your professional judgment.

I know what your first reaction is likely to be because all of us have been in that position at one time or another. I admit that I used to smile indulgently on those occasions and murmur something like, "Well, you know how *those* books are. By the way, have you been remembering to take your medicine regularly?" But this book is different—and not because I wrote it. To be honest, you could have written the same book— maybe even a better one—because we all have access to the same technical and scientific material. I happened to write it because I am convinced that implementing the high-fiber diet has immense positive potential as a powerful tool of preventive medicine, especially in those areas where our ability to cure the patient is so limited.

I consider this such a vital question that I am going to ask you to do me one small favor—before you make up your mind, and your patients' minds, on this most important issue.

Please ask your medical librarian to provide you with reprints of the following two articles:

1. "Dietary Fiber and Disease," *Journal of the American Medical Association,* August 19, 1974, Vol. 229, No. 8, pp. 1068–1074.
2. "Roughage in the Diet," *Medical World News,* September 6, 1974, pp. 35–42.

If you'd rather not impose on the librarian, simply write the word "Fiber" on your professional card and mail it to me at the following address:

Dr. David Reuben
c/o Random House
201 East 50th Street
New York, N.Y. 10022

I'll make sure you get the reprints by return mail.
Then read them over and decide whether, in your considered professional opinion, the risk-reward ratio justifies these simple additions to the diet, on a trial basis, of patients with markedly elevated cholesterol, a strong family history of cancer of the colon or rectum, diverticulosis, or some of the other conditions mentioned.
If you have any questions at that point, simply write to me and I'll be happy to try and answer them personally.
Thanks for taking the time to read this.

Fraternally yours,

David Reuben, M.D.

David Reuben, M.D.

DRR/cg

Why I Wrote This Book

For five years I watched my father die slowly of cancer of the colon. I made sure he had the finest doctors in the country and the most advanced treatment available. It didn't make any difference because the slow-growing cancer relentlessly destroyed him. No one could tell me the cause of his malignancy, no one could tell me how it could have been prevented, and the best treatment modern medicine could offer was essentially the same as that used in 1900. The surgeons cut out the tumor and most of his large intestine; they relocated his anus in his lower abdomen, which caused him great emotional trauma. In spite of devoted doctors and massive medical costs, he died.

Four years ago, I noticed a small article in one of the medical journals suggesting that restoring roughage to the modern diet might be beneficial in treating constipation, hemorrhoids, and "irritable colon"—three conditions that are annoying but hardly life-threatening. But I also knew that these three conditions have at least a statistical correlation with cancer of the colon. So I followed up the article, and for the past four years I have read nearly every bit of scientific material written on the role of roughage in human disease. I am now convinced that not only could my father's life have been saved, but millions of other cancer victims would be alive today if they had simply been able to add a few cents' worth of vegetable fiber to their daily diet.

I must admit that when I first began my research I had the usual physician's skepticism. The articles—even in the medical journals—seemed reminiscent of those advocating wheat germ, blackstrap molasses, and yogurt. But now that over six hundred unassailable articles have been published in respected medical journals around the world confirming and reconfirming the validity of the findings, there seems little doubt that adding the missing roughage to our daily diet provides protection from:

1. Cancer of the colon and rectum.

2. Ischemic heart disease—*the prime cause of heart attacks*.

3. Diverticular disease of the colon.

4. Appendicitis.

5. Phlebitis and resulting blood clots to the lungs.

6. *Obesity*.

I know that this sounds like the claims on a bottle of Vegetable Tonic—and that worried me until I saw each element of protection validated and revalidated in the most rigorously scientific way.

This is the most exciting medical story of the 1970's—and I feel that by telling it simply, directly, and honestly I can benefit a lot of people—although unfortunately not my father.

Acknowledgments

I would like to thank my friend and agent, Don Congdon, for his encouragement and enthusiasm—as always. Anne Tiffany made many burdens lighter. The American Medical Association Medical Library and their able staff of research librarians were indispensable, as well as the Medical Library at the University of Miami and its staff. I also want to thank the library staff and the administrator of the Naples Community Hospital, Bill Crone.

Carol Lundequist did an outstanding job of preparing the manuscript on Sparky's Magic Typewriter.

The munchkins, as usual, made it all worthwhile.

Honor Roll

The following distinguished scientists have made valuable contributions to the discovery and understanding of the role of dietary fiber in the prevention and treatment of disease:

Dr. Denis Burkitt	Dr. A. R. Short
Dr. Martin Eastwood	Dr. Peter Plumley
Dr. Kenneth Heaton	Brian Francis
Dr. Thomas Cleave	Dr. Anthony Almeida
Dr. Hubert Trowell	Dr. Kenneth Colebourne
Dr. Neil Painter	Dr. Peter James
Dr. Joseph Piepmeyer	Dr. A. Antonis
Dr. A. R. P. Walker	Dr. I. Bersohn
Dr. J. M. Hinton	

I realize of course that this is only a partial list and if anyone will bring any missing names to my attention, I will be sure they are included in the next edition.

Contents

1

How to Prevent Heart Attacks and the Major Forms of Cancer

Consider a medical Garden of Eden. Imagine a society where heart attacks don't exist, where the two major forms of death-dealing cancer are virtually unknown, where phlebitis and the resulting blood clots in the lungs are almost unheard of. Think of a world where many of the petty ailments of modern society have been virtually eliminated—appendicitis, hemorrhoids, obesity, diverticulosis of the colon, and varicose veins. Is this the United States in the year 2500?

No. It's rural Africa in the year 1975. It's a society and a way of life that has *almost completely avoided the major scourges of the modern world*. Most important of all, buried in the tribal life of these Africans is a secret that can make a better life for nearly every man and woman in America.

We all know—from the yearly newspaper stories—that life expectancy in the United States has increased dramatically in the past fifty years. But few of us know how deceptive these statistics are. It's *not* because our general health is improving—it's merely because fewer children now die before the age of five. (Life-expectancy calculations use a complex formula based on age at death of those who die each year to arrive at an expectancy figure for those still living. As more children survive longer—due to antibiotics, immunization, and better sanitation—the overall figure of "life expectancy" is deceptively increased.)

Actually, in some years even the official figure has been declining. The basic reason for that decline is that as each year passes, more Americans succumb to the two great destroyers—cancer and heart attacks. In addition, obesity, diverticular disease, and high blood pressure are also increasing. Worst of all, modern medicine seems to be helpless in stemming the tide. The basic treatment of cancer has not changed since 1900—wait until the wildly multiplying cells take over part of the body and then desperately try to destroy the tissues or the organ they have invaded. The survival rates from cancer mirror our impotence.

FIVE-YEAR SURVIVAL RATES FOR VARIOUS TYPES
OF CANCER
(Assuming regional involvement)

The following figures indicate the percentage for patients who will be alive five years after their cancer has been treated to the limit of our current knowledge:

Prostate: 57%	Larynx: 38%
Breast: 56%	Mouth: 30%
Uterus: 44%	Bladder: 21%
Colon & Rectum: 43%	Lung: 10%

(Based on figures from End Results Group, National Cancer Institute)

IMPORTANT NOTICE: According to the latest information just released by the American Cancer Society,* cancer of the colon and rectum has now taken over first place as *the most common form of lethal cancer in the United States.* Over 99,000 new cases of colon

---

* National Cancer Institute, Third National Cancer Survey.

and rectum cancer occur in our nation each year, resulting in more than 49,000 deaths. That means that on the average someone develops this form of cancer *every five minutes,* and every ten minutes *someone dies from it.*

These shocking new figures make it even more urgent for everyone to take prompt action to restore the essential roughage to their daily diet.

In spite of spending billions on research and shiny electronic equipment, we are still helpless to prevent heart attacks in any meaningful way. We don't even know how to effectively *treat* a heart-attack victim—all medical science can offer is rest and measures to limit the damage and avoid complications. The same applies to the other killers—high blood pressure, diverticulosis, obesity, and blood clots in the deep veins of the legs and lungs. Cause: unknown. Treatment: directed at symptoms, not at the basic cause. (The treatment for high blood pressure lowers the pressure, treatment for blood clots tries to dissolve the clots, treatment for obesity tries to suppress the appetite. But none of those are the *underlying causes* of the conditions.)

In a tale that has all the excitement and suspense of a mystery story, a small group of British scientists has made a series of discoveries that promises to remove —once and for all—these crippling and deadly diseases as threats to the health of our nation—and the entire world. The tracking of clues extends all the way from analyzing the lunch menu in an African village to studying bakery recipes in an English mill town in 1850. Prosaically, it all began with an observation about the bowel movements of African villagers.[1] English doctors working among the natives noticed that the Africans passed about one pound of fecal material per day.[2] This was a startling contrast to the normal English bowel movement of less than four ounces! There were other differences: The Africans' feces were bulky, soft and almost completely odor-free; the British bowel movements were hard and compressed, and had a rotten, putrified odor.[3] To the average person a bowel movement is a source of embarrassment, the butt of infantile jokes, and the object of almost compulsive cleanliness. But to a physician the feces are an important source of information about one of the most essential functions of the human body —digestion. Everything that happens to your body —or is going to happen to it—is dependent on the process of converting what you consume into the cells, tissues, and organs of your body.

The process of digestion is complicated and still poorly understood in comparison to some other less important bodily processes. However, there are some highlights that are especially significant.

The processing of the food you eat, from the mouth through the stomach and intestines, is very similar to a mining process. If you consider your daily diet to be the raw ore, the goal of digestion is to extract the fat, protein, carbohydrates, vitamins, and minerals that your organism needs. Once that is accomplished, the sludge or tailings from the refining process must be disposed of. Scientists always considered this to be the least important part of the digestive process. In the colon or large intestine, water is absorbed, bacteria act on the residue (as a matter of fact, up to 30 percent of feces are composed of bacteria), and the powerful muscles of the colon compress the mass like a gigantic trash compacter. The resulting fecal contents are then expelled.

The medical investigators knew all that, but they were at a loss to explain why the Africans should produce four times as much fecal mass, odor-free and consistently soft and bulky.

Their next discovery was even more puzzling—the food consumed by the Africans went from the dinner table to the bowel movement in as little as twenty-four hours![4] The average Englishman retained what he ate for a full three days, and some individual Britons took up to two weeks to fully process their food.[5]

Intrigued by these findings, the researchers pressed on. They began to analyze the daily diets of the rural Africans and made even more fascinating discoveries —discoveries that may open the door to freedom from incalculable suffering and expense for millions of people. The average village dweller ate a diet that was pitiful by our standards. He consumed corn meal, beans, bananas, and potatoes. His daily food ration was notable in only one regard: it was extremely high in vegetable fiber. That's the part of plant material people eat but are unable to completely digest. It includes most of the things that stick in your teeth, make chewing hard and vegetables unpleasant to consume: things like the bran on the wheat berry, the strings in string beans, part of the oats in rolled oats, the skins of apples and potatoes, and all the rest. Because the Africans consumed so much of this fiber or "roughage," their food fairly raced through their digestive system. That much was interesting but certainly not exciting. When the Britishers summarized their findings, this was what they had:

1. Africans had more massive, heavier, less odoriferous bowel movements than Englishmen.

2. Africans moved their food through the body three times faster than Englishmen.

3. Africans ate about three times as much roughage or vegetable fiber as Englishmen.

That would have been material for an obscure article in a minor medical journal except—fortunately for the world—the British doctors didn't stop there. They began to look for other differences between the supposedly "deprived" Africans and their much more affluent English counterparts. What they found may be about to revolutionize modern medicine. Their discovery, I believe, is potentially more valuable than much of the multibillion-dollar medical research conducted over the past half-century. Their simple observations may save millions from the pain and suffering and death of heart attacks and cancer and avoid tens of billions of dollars' worth of surgery, hospital stays, and therapy.

After a painstaking analysis of countless medical records—comparing death and illness rates for various groups—this is what the researchers found:

1. Coronary heart disease, the cause of heart attacks which are *responsible for one-third of all deaths in the United States,* is virtually *unknown* in rural Africa.[6]

2. Cancer of the colon and rectum, the number one form of lethal cancer in the United States, is extremely rare in country-dwelling Africans.[7-8]

3. Appendicitis, *the most common abdominal surgical emergency in the United States,* is almost never encountered among African villagers.[9]

4. Hemorrhoids, that scourge of civilization, the cause of untold suffering and disability, is extremely rare among those eating the traditional African diet.[10]

5. Among Americans, diverticulosis (big pockets pouching out in the wall of the large intestine) is the most common disease of the colon; half of older Americans are its victims. Africans almost never get it.[11]

6. Ten percent of all Americans have varicose veins. It is very unusual for a rural African to have this condition.[12]

7. Phlebitis is an everyday cause of illness and suffering among Americans. Phlebitis (blood clots

in the deep veins of the legs) is potentially lethal since the clots can shoot upward into the lungs and cause sudden death. Africans rarely are afflicted by this condition.[13]

8.   Obesity, that disabling and disfiguring condition, to some degree affects half of our population. Africans who adhere to their traditional diet *do not become obese*.[14,15]

It was almost too much for sophisticated minds to absorb. Could it be that the simple, almost inadequate diet of the Africans saved them from the half-dozen or so diseases that kill or cripple millions in North America and Europe? Could it be that our diet—packed with protein, enriched with vitamins and minerals, safeguarded by government standards—could be so deficient in some vital factor that it is filling our hospitals and cemeteries with victims of cancer and heart attacks? Is it possible that one-third of a million American doctors, dedicated to removing cancerous organs, ministering to heart-attack victims, and operating on appendicitis, varicose veins, hemorrhoids, and diverticulosis could someday devote their attention to practicing the *preventive medicine* they all agree is more rewarding?

These questions had to be answered once and for all—not on the basis of wishful thinking, but by objective analysis of scientific facts. Maybe the observation that rural Africans were spared so much illness while the health of "modern" society was deteriorating could be explained on the basis of heredity. Perhaps there was something in the genes of black Africans that provided them with immunity to these terrible diseases. The researchers continued their investigations. More tedious analysis of medical records around the world produced these findings:

1.   Africans who adopt a *Western diet* gradually develop *Western diseases*. Obviously it takes some

time for the conditions to become manifest, although appendicitis shows up first in Africans who drastically cut the amount of roughage in their diets. Gradually cancer of the colon, heart attacks, diverticulosis, and all the rest of the grim illnesses begin to follow.[16]

2. Black Africans who come to the United States and adopt an American diet slowly succumb to these degenerative diseases. Within about thirty years the conditions begin to appear in alarming numbers.[17,18]

Trying to explain the difference in susceptibility in terms of Negroid-Caucasian racial differences led up a blind alley in another respect. Native Japanese on a traditional diet are nearly as free from these conditions as African blacks. But when Japanese move to Hawaii and adopt a low-roughage diet there, they slowly begin to develop heart attacks and colon cancer in increasing amounts, along with the rest of the diseases mentioned.[19] Another bit of confirmatory evidence comes from the "Westernized" Japanese who still live in Japan but have adopted an American-style low-fiber diet. Their illness and death rate inevitably follows the American pattern.[20]

Even Caucasians like Turks and Romanians relentlessly begin to succumb to the fiber deficiency diseases shortly after they relinquish their high-roughage traditional diets and eat the way we do.[21]

Spurred on by these vital discoveries, the medical researchers began to analyze the modern American and British diets. What they found was an amazing chronicle of how so-called progress extracts its price. At the same time they discovered the means of potentially sparing all of us the disease and disability that has become an almost inevitable consequence of our way of life.

Notes

1. A. R. P. Walker (1947). "The Effect of Recent Changes of Food Habits on Bowel Motility." *South African Medical Journal* 21: 590–596.
2. D. P. Burkitt (1971). "Diverticular Disease of the Colon; A Deficiency Disease of Western Civilization." *British Medical Journal* 2: 450–454.
3. T. L. Cleave *et al.* (1969). *Diabetes, Coronary Thrombosis and the Saccharine Diseases,* 2nd ed. Bristol: John Wright and Sons, Ltd.
4. J. M. Hinton *et al.* (1969). "A New Method for Studying Gut Transit Times Using Radio-Opaque Markers." *Journal of the British Society of Gastroenterology* 10: 842–847.
5. J. C. Brocklehurst *et al.* (1969). *Gerontologica Clinica* 2: 293.
6. V. Schire (1971). "Heart Disease in Southern Africa with Special Reference to Ischaemic Heart Disease." *South African Medical Journal* 45: 634–644.
7. R. Doll (1960). "The Geographical Incidence of Cancer." *British Journal of Cancer* 23: 1–8.
8. R. Doll *et al.* (1966). *Cancer Incidence in Five Continents* (UICC Report). Heidelberg: Springer-Verlag.
9. A. R. P. Walker *et al.* (1973). "Appendicitis, Fibre Intake and Bowel Behaviour in Ethnic Groups in South Africa." *Postgraduate Medical Journal* 49: 243–249.
10. D. P. Burkitt (1972). "Varicose Veins, Deep Vein Thrombosis, and Haemorrhoids: Epidemiology and Suggested Aetiology." *British Medical Journal* 2:556–561.
11. N. S. Painter *et al.* (1971). "Diverticular Disease of the Colon: A Deficiency Disease of Western Civilization." *British Medical Journal* 2: 450–454.
12. See note 10 above.

13. See note 3 above.
14. N. A. Scotch (1960). "A Preliminary Report on the Relation of Socio-Cultural Factors to Hypertension among the Zulu." *Annals of the New York Academy of Science* 84: 1000–1009.
15. A. R. P. Walker (1964). "Overweight and Hypertension in Emerging Populations (editorial)." *American Heart Journal* 68: 581–585.
16. P. E. Steiner (1954). *Cancer, Race, and Geography.* Baltimore, Maryland: Williams and Wilkins Co.
17. W. S. Quinland (1940). "Primary Carcinoma in the Negro." *Archives of Pathology* 30: 393–402.
18. E. J. Kocour (1937). "Diverticulosis of the Colon." *American Journal of Surgery* 37: 430–436.
19. G. N. Stemmermann (1970). "Patterns of Disease among Japanese Living in Hawaii." *Archives of Environmental Health* 20: 266–273.
20. E. L. Wynder *et al.* (1967). "Environmental Factors of Cancer of the Colon and Rectum." *Cancer* 20: 1520–1561.
21. D. P. D. Wilkie (1914). *British Medical Journal* 2: 959.

2

The One Deficiency in Our Modern Diet That Is Killing Us

As the original findings of those on-the-scene medical researchers were published in international medical journals, other scientists around the world turned their attention to the relationship between the epidemic of degenerative diseases and the diet of modern, urban men and women.

What they discovered was a shocking indictment of current nutritional practices. In effect, modern diets are glaringly deficient in that single substance that is very likely related to a long and disease-free life. To put it bluntly, affluent Americans (and other Westerners) are eating a high-priced, high-prestige diet that leads them directly to cancer of the colon, heart attacks, obesity, and hypertension. In addition, the greater part of what were considered the burdens of civilization—hemorrhoids, varicose veins, diverticulosis, "irritable colon," appendicitis, and others—are *simply the result of a deficient diet*.

There are two obstacles to understanding which can occur at this point. First, how can a diet that is as rich and as varied as the typical American diet possibly be deficient?

The answer to that is this: our diet is neither as rich nor as varied as it might appear. The bulk of our intake nowadays consists of extensively purified carbohydrate —mainly starches and sugars—as well as substantial amounts of fats and oils. To a diner there is a big difference between a sweet roll and a bowl of pre-sweetened cereal, but to the gastrointestinal system, they are nearly identical. Instant mashed potatoes seem quite a different dish from a plateful of white rice, but from a nutritional point of view they are almost identical.

The second question is: "How can a single deficiency be responsible for diseases as different from one another as heart attacks, cancer of the colon, diverticular disease of the colon, and hemorrhoids?" The answer: each of those conditions is directly related to the digestion and metabolism of food and the operation of the digestive system. As the story unfolds we will be able to consider the far-reaching evidence that conclusively proves this point. But first let's go back a century in time to examine the missing pieces in the dietary puzzle:

In the Western world about 1880 a strange obsession began to appear. For some years before that time men of wealth, aristocrats, and, of course, royalty had eaten nothing but white bread. The peasants and poor city dwellers were compelled to settle for "black" bread, which was made from coarsely milled flour. Presumably consumers rated their bread on a "prestige scale"—white bread was considered "pure" and dark bread, containing substantial amounts of roughage, was considered "impure." The flour mills then used stone grinding wheels, and since their surfaces were rough, no matter how well they were positioned, the wheat berries could not be smashed completely. Even carefully ground wheat flour still contained a fair amount of bran and other fiber. (Flour that was whitened by sifting through cloths was a high-cost item for the rich.[1])

But in the 1880's there was a revolution in the milling industry: the steel rolling mill was introduced. Since the precisely polished steel surfaces mated perfectly, the grains of wheat could be smashed finer than ever before. That enabled millers to easily extract most of the fiber and produce a low-cost, high-prestige, nearly pure-white flour.[2,3,4] The new roller mills also had an important incidental advantage. One of the annoyances of the flour trade was the relatively high loss of stored wheat to insects. The ultra-refined flour had so much of the nutrient material removed that it was barely able to sustain life in bugs—therefore insect infestation was reduced considerably. The irony of feeding men, women, and children with flour that hardly kept bugs alive was lost on those early millers.

Those changes in milling practices were critical to the health of the average person, since in the nineteenth century the individual consumed about one pound of flour a day—mostly in the form of bread. (These days the average person eats about six ounces of flour daily.) [5,6,7]

At the same time that most of the fiber was taken out of the flour, the consumption of sugar began to increase. Going back to 1815, the average Englishman consumed about ten pounds of sugar *a year*; his American cousin, somewhat less. By 1965 he was taking in *one hundred and twenty pounds* yearly, or his previous total annual consumption *every month*.[8] One problem with sugar from the standpoint of the fiber-deficiency diseases is that it contains no fiber at all. At the same time, it is so filling that it cuts down the appetite for roughage-containing foods.

As time went by, more and more of the diet of Western man has come to consist of sugar in various forms combined with white-flour products such as ultra-refined bread, cereals, doughnuts, cakes, pies, cookies, instant potatoes, and white rice. There seem to have been some beneficial changes in the diet in that period—at least at first glance. The average consumption of roughage-containing fruit and vegetables in 1909 was about 146 pounds per person per year. By 1970 that had increased to 273 pounds yearly. Unfortunately much of the fiber content has been lost by peeling, boiling, canning, dehydrating, and otherwise processing that category of food. In addition, we tend to consume new strains of low-fiber fruits and vegetables adapted to modern taste—some examples being the "stringless" string bean and the "burpless" cucumber.[9,10]

To medical researchers, the mass of evidence now seemed to implicate the modern low-roughage diet as an important cause of the serious diseases of modern civilization. Nutritionists and scientists all over the world became more and more intrigued. But there was one important loophole in the evidence that needed to be plugged before the facts could be considered conclusive. If a deficiency of fiber or roughage was to be proved responsible for the massive increase in lethal and destructive diseases, then simply comparing the health of the rural Africans with the health of Western man was not enough. The ultimate confirmation would come if it were possible to show that as the dietary fiber was removed from the Western diet—as we ate less roughage—we began to succumb to these terrible afflictions. The search for that confirmatory evidence set off a minutely detailed examination of medical records around the world. Based on the fact that the substantial reduction of roughage in flour began about 1880, this is what the researchers found:

1. Heart attacks—which we accept as a daily occurrence—were *extremely rare in the United States and Britain until about the 1920's*. Then suddenly from 1931 to 1971 in England and Wales coronary heart disease—the cause of heart attacks—increased *800 percent!* [11]

2. Appendicitis—the disease that shows up some twenty to thirty years before the other, more deadly effects of a roughage-deficient diet—was very rare before 1880. Subsequently it gradually assumed epidemic proportions.[12,13]

3. Diverticular disease of the colon only emerged as a common disease in the late 1920's. In Britain, between 1931 and 1971 the death rate from that condition increased *600 percent!* [14]

4. Even obesity, which we take for granted as part of our modern way of life, was a disease that generally affected only the wealthy in eighteenth-century Europe.[15]

These are only the most outstanding and dramatic examples. Painstaking review of the medical records reveals that the same general evolution applies to each of the major conditions. There are millions of individual bits of evidence in dozens of countries around the world that confirm and reconfirm the basic premise: *As the amount of roughage in the diet decreases, the incidence of heart attacks, cancer of the colon and rectum, diverticulosis of the colon, and all the rest increase in almost direct proportion.* In each case— except for the standard-bearer, appendicitis, which appears earlier—there seems to be a time lag of about fifty years—enough time for the body to lose its natural defenses and undergo a certain amount of deterioration in function.[16]

By the time all this evidence was in, our modern fiber-deficient diet was almost unanimously indicted as the basic cause of these death- and disability-dealing diseases by international medical experts.

To recapitulate, the chain of evidence was as follows:

1. The aforementioned diseases are virtually unknown in those individuals and cultures consuming a high-roughage diet.

2. They are catastrophically common in individuals and societies where the diet is low in roughage or dietary fiber.

19

3. When high-roughage individuals or groups switch to low-roughage diets they gradually but relentlessly succumb to these diseases.

A close look at the typical American diet gives some idea of the extent of the hazard. Let's take three average American meals and rate them for their fiber content and sugar content:

BREAKFAST:

Orange flavored breakfast drink (Tang or equivalent)	High refined sugar Zero fiber
White bread toasted with butter and jelly	Moderate sugar Very low fiber
Two eggs, any style	Zero fiber
Coffee with sugar	Moderate refined sugar Zero fiber

LUNCH:

Sandwich with assorted luncheon meat on white bread	Very low fiber
Soft drink	High refined sugar
Lettuce salad	Low to moderate fiber

DINNER:

Roast beef, mashed potatoes, frozen peas	Low to moderate fiber
Coleslaw	Moderate fiber
White bread	Near zero fiber
Ice cream	Zero fiber High refined sugar

If those three meals are consumed on Monday, the complete processing and digestion will be concluded, on the average, by late Wednesday, and the residual material from the menu will be passed in a small, hard, constipated bowel movement on Friday morning. *If the same American family had consumed a readily available high-fiber equivalent diet on the same day, the food would have been completely processed by the next morning and all the residual products eliminated by Tuesday at the latest.* Ironically, the high-roughage diet (as we shall see) is more appetizing, less expensive, more satisfying, and more conducive to weight reduction than its low-roughage equivalent.

Even more tantalizing is the tiny amount of fiber that makes the difference between the possibility of cancer, heart attacks and all the rest and the almost total immunity enjoyed by those on high-fiber diets. On the average African villagers consume slightly less than *one ounce* (25 grams) of fiber per day.[17] Modern Americans and Britons consume about *one-quarter ounce* of fiber daily (8 grams).[18,19] The balance between potential health and potential disease is tipped by three-quarters of an ounce of almost indigestible fibrous material costing, at the most, two cents a day. On a yearly basis, twelve pounds of roughage added to the average diet at a total cost of a little over seven dollars provides a million dollars' worth of life and health insurance.

Is there any risk involved in adding roughage to the usual roughage-deficient diet? It's hard to see what the risk might be, since we are only restoring the diet to what it was for the 50,000 years up to about 1880. Man, left to his own instinct, had naturally chosen a high-fiber non-fattening diet that encouraged the natural and normal functioning of his digestive system and protected him from the most horrendous diseases of "modern" civilization.

But to convict the fiber-deficient diet once and for all, one last loophole has to be closed. We need to demonstrate exactly how low-roughage diets do their terrible damage and show how high-roughage diets restore and maintain the body in a state of maximum health. The simplest and most objective way to judge the evidence is to examine what goes on in the human body day after day. Let's start at the beginning of the story—the digestive system.

Notes

1. M. A. Antar *et al.* (1964). "Perspectives in Nutrition." *American Journal of Clinical Nutrition* 14: 169–178.
2. J. Robertson (1972). "Changes in the Fibre Content of the British Diet." *Nature* (London) 238: 290–292.
3. N. L. Kent (1970). *Technology of Cereals.* Oxford: Pergamon Press.
4. D. F. Hollingsworth *et al.* (1967). "Consumption of Carbohydrates in the United Kingdom." *American Journal of Clinical Nutrition* 20: 65–72.
5. E. M. W. Lloyd (1936). "Food Supplies and Consumption of Different Income Levels." *Journal of the Proceedings of the Agricultural Economics Society* 4: 89–120.
6. J. Levi *et al.* (1882). In *Report of the Fifty-first Meeting of the British Association for the Advancement of Science* (1881), London, n.p., pp. 272–289.
7. C. R. Jones (1958). "The Essentials of the Flour Milling Process." *Proceedings of the Nutrition Society* 17: 7–15.
8. See note 1 above.
9. See note 2 above.
10. J. P. Greaves *et al.* (1966). "Trends in Food Consumption in the United Kingdom." *World Review of Nutrition and Dietetics* 6: 34–89.
11. *Medical World News,* "Roughage in the Diet," September 6, 1974, pp. 35–42.
12. A. R. Short (1920). "The Causation of Appendicitis." *British Journal of Surgery* 8: 171–186.

13. T. L. Cleave *et al.* (1969). *Diabetes, Coronary Thrombosis, and the Saccharine Diseases,* 2nd ed. Bristol: John Wright and Sons, Ltd.
14. See note 11 above.
15. D. P. Burkitt. "Dietary Fiber and Disease." *Journal of the American Medical Association* 229: 1068–1074.
16. D. P. Burkitt (1972). "Effect of Dietary Fibre on Stools and Transit Times and Its Role in the Causation of Disease." *Lancet* 2: 1408–1411.
17. A. M. Lubbe (1971). "A Comparative Study of Rural and Urban Venda Males: Dietary Evaluation." *South African Medical Journal* 45: 1289–1297.
18. See note 2 above.
19. M. G. Hardinge *et al.* (1958). "Nutritional Studies of Vegetarians: III. Dietary Levels of Fiber." *American Journal of Clinical Nutrition* 6: 523–525.

3

How the Wrong Diet Can Cause Cancer of the Colon and Rectum and Exactly How to Avoid It

The process of digestion is one of the true miracles of the universe. Everything an individual consumes passes through about forty feet of complicated gastrointestinal tubing and is acted upon by approximately two dozen chemical compounds. In the process such diverse dishes as frog's legs, calves' brains, oxtails, and pig's feet are converted to the basic building blocks of the human body. Briefly, this is the way the process works:

Once the food is chewed and swallowed, it passes into the stomach, where it is mixed with hydrochloric acid and digestive chemicals. It then passes into the small intestine—twenty-three feet of relatively small-diameter flexible pipe. Secretions from the liver are added, via the gall bladder, and other enzymes are secreted by the pancreas. By this time the food is well mashed and uniformly mixed with the digestive chemicals. Although some absorption may have occurred in the stomach, the major part of the nutrition is extracted from the food in the small intestine. Then the mushy mass of almost totally digested food is pushed into the colon. As far as most students of nutrition are concerned, that's when the game is over. As far as we are concerned, that's when things *really* get interesting.

For all too many years the five or so feet of the large intestine or colon were considered to be the sewage disposal plant of the body. The colon was viewed as a sort of septic tank to hold fecal material between bowel movements. As a result of many years of ingenious and sophisticated research it has now become obvious that the colon may play a vital role in the destiny of the human organism.

Instead of a stagnant holding tank, the colon is actually a living river. The dregs of digestion (feces is the plural of the Latin word *faex*, which means "dregs") are half liquid and half solid, and flow through the colon like an active stream. The solid portion of the fecal material precedes the liquid part and the wall of the intestine selectively soaks up excess water.

For hundreds of years people have instinctively felt that there was something vaguely undesirable about allowing those dregs to accumulate day after day in that large flexible tunnel deep in the abdomen. Our grandparents prescribed "high enemas" or "colonic irrigations" to dispose of fecal accumulations. Even today there is a billion-dollar sale of laxatives designed to empty the colon of its contents. (An interesting fringe benefit of the extensive research on the effects of roughage showed the undesirability of taking laxatives for this purpose and even indicated that one type of commonly prescribed laxative can destroy the nerves that control the large intestine.) Without knowing why, our old-fashioned forebears were on the right track. One of the greatest risks a human being can take is to allow the remnants of his food—that is, the fecal end products—to remain in contact with the lining of his colon for three and four days at a time. And that's exactly what 99 percent of Americans and others who eat a "modern" diet are doing. At the end of their digestive tract they are harboring a time bomb. This is what the researchers in laboratories around the world found:

Every cancer researcher agrees that cancer can be caused by body surfaces coming in contact with potent cancer-causing chemicals known as *carcinogens*. Unfortunately, there are examples all around us. Vinyl chloride as a cause of fatal cancer of the liver has gotten a great deal of publicity lately. Many of the food additives that have recently been banned are known or suspected to have caused cancer in human beings. The actual list of cancer-producing chemicals contains many hundreds of items, most of them organic chemicals with exotic names like methyl cholanthrene and the like.

In the process of studying cancer of the colon in rats, one investigator made a startling discovery. He fed a drug called cycasin to a group of normal rats. As expected, many of them promptly developed cancer of the colon. Then, on impulse, he tried the same experiment with a group of special rats who had been raised in such a way that their bodies were absolutely free of bacteria. To his amazement, none of the bacteria-free rats developed cancer. He then went on to analyze the urine and feces from both groups of rats, and what he found has life-and-death implications for two hundred million Americans. In the germ-free —and thus cancer-free—rats, the cancer-producing drug cycasin was recovered unchanged in the urine and feces. But in the cancer-ridden rats, only 35 percent of the chemical, at the most, was found in those waste products. That meant that the bacteria in the colon of the cancerous rats had broken down the cycasin into powerful, cancer-causing chemicals.[1,2]

Turning their attention to human beings, scientists made a parallel and even more astonishing discovery. The human liver normally produces a chemical combination that we call *bile*. It is a thick greenish liquid essential for digestion, especially for the breakdown of fats. Bile is composed of several different chemicals known as *bile acids* that go by such arcane names as cholic acid and deoxycholic acid. (Incidentally, it is the pigments of bile that give feces their brownish color. If for some reason the liver is obstructed, as in hepatitis, bile cannot enter the small intestine and the bowel movement becomes pale, almost white, in color. The pigment may find its way into the skin and turn it greenish-yellow, causing jaundice.)

In any event, the investigators found that the average low-roughage-consuming American has two nutritionally significant types of bacteria in his colon; the dominant group is known as *bacteroides* and *bifidobacteria*.[8] It has been proved beyond any doubt that the bile acid cholic acid can be converted into the powerful cancer-causing chemical apcholic acid. Likewise the other bile acid, deoxycholic acid, can be changed into one of the most potent known carcinogens, *3-methyl-cholanthrene*.

The implications of those discoveries are simple and unequivocal: *Americans who are on lifelong low-roughage diets are probably converting their own harmless bile acids into awesome cancer-producing compounds within the confines of their own large intestines.*[4,5]

Further proof lies in the fact that individuals on low-roughage diets pass decreased amounts of bile acids in their bowel movements, indicating that, like cancerous rats, they have broken them down into carcinogenic compounds. On the other hand, those persons who consume high-roughage diets have a colon dominated by streptococus and lactobacillus bacteria, which do not appear to attack the bile acids and break them down. As additional confirmation of this protection, high-roughage individuals pass a much greater proportion of *intact, unchanged* bile acids in their feces.[6] Assuming that these potentially lethal chemicals are accumulating in the colon as each day passes, the body's next line of defense is to get them out of contact with the soft and vulnerable lining of the large intestine. Ironically, only those on high-roughage diets—who are never exposed to the cancer chemicals —don't have to worry on that score. They store their freshest fecal products in the colon for less than eighteen hours on the average, based on the fact that special markers pass through their *entire* digestive tracts in about twenty-four hours.[7]

The low-roughage carcinogen-producing American diet allows the fecal mass and its store of cancer chemicals to wash over the colon for seventy-two hours or longer—and in the case of some British patients, for as long as two weeks.[8] Even our valuable and dedicated astronauts are deliberately fed a special low-roughage diet which delays their bowel movements as long as six days. (Cancer of the colon seems a high price to pay for the exploration of space.)

Beyond that, each bowel movement consists of 20 to 30 percent bacteria—so the faster any bile-acid-splitting bacteria are moved out of the intestine, the less mischief they can perform.

Other experiments leave little doubt that encouraging prolonged contact between the remnants of digestion and the wall of the colon is inviting disaster. In those experimental animals who are deliberately given cancer, simply isolating a loop of intestine so that feces never flow over it prevents malignant changes in that isolated loop.[9] There is a further fascinating observation made by a leading researcher: For all practical purposes, only two epithelial-lined channels are common sites of cancer—the bronchial tubes, which are the location of the most common form of lung cancer, and the colon. These are—not by co-incidence—the only channels or tubes that are exposed to foreign substances. The bronchial tubes are exposed to cigarette smoke and the colon is exposed to the slow-moving fecal stream containing residual carcinogenic chemicals from unnaturally low-roughage foods.

The irony of being an unwilling accomplice in the development of one's own colon cancer is compounded by the fact that modern therapy for cancer of that organ is not really encouraging. In fact, it has not basically changed since 1900. The strategy is to wait helplessly until the cancer is firmly established within your large intestine. You will know the time has arrived when you have pain, bleeding, diarrhea, or constipation. Then, as the cancer is growing day by day, medical science finally makes a dedicated and valiant effort to save your life.

The actual treatment of the malignant tumor is based on destroying the affected part of the organ as well as a sizable amount of healthy tissue. In many cases of cancer of the colon (and the extension of the colon, the rectum), that means closing off the anus and repositioning it permanently in the abdominal wall. In some cases, tumor tissue (and an unavoidable amount of normal tissue) is destroyed by radiation—similar to the fallout from a nuclear explosion. Patients are also treated on occasion by chemotherapy—that is, the administration of extremely toxic drugs designed to kill tumor cells without damaging the patient's body permanently. Tragically, in spite of the Herculean efforts of devoted specialists, barely half of those stricken with colon cancer survive. How much better it would be to simply add roughage to one's diet and drastically reduce the risk of ever succumbing to colon cancer.

Unfortunately, the risk for Americans is a very real one. The United States has nearly the highest rate of colon cancer in the world. About 42 out of every 100,000 American men between the ages of thirty-five and sixty-four develop cancer of the colon and rectum. In some areas of the country the risk is even greater. For example, in the state of Connecticut, the rate is 52 per 100,000, and the state of New York has a rate of 46 per 100,000. It seems more than a coincidence that our national diet is nearly the lowest in roughage of any nation in the world. By contrast, the incidence of colon cancer in the United States is *900 percent greater* than that of Nigeria and *1,300 percent greater* than Uganda, two countries with traditional high-roughage diets.[10]

Although rural African blacks are protected from

cancer of the colon by their high-roughage diet, that immunity does not extend to their American cousins. After two generations of living in the United States and gradually shifting to a low-fiber diet, the rate for colon cancer among black Americans is almost identical to that of their white fellow citizens.[11] That's exactly what one would expect, since both black and white digestive systems now operate in deadly slow motion. The same misfortune has befallen second-generation Japanese who have moved to Hawaii and the U.S. and forsaken the traditional Japanese high-fiber diet.[12] The rate of colon malignancy is also rising

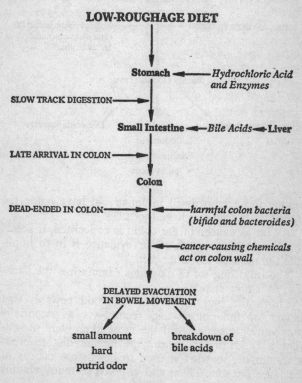

LOW-ROUGHAGE DIET

Stomach ⟵ *Hydrochloric Acid and Enzymes*

SLOW TRACK DIGESTION ⟶

Small Intestine ⟵ *Bile Acids* ⟵ **Liver**

LATE ARRIVAL IN COLON ⟶

Colon

DEAD-ENDED IN COLON ⟶ ⟵ *harmful colon bacteria (bifido and bacteroides)*

⟵ *cancer-causing chemicals act on colon wall*

DELAYED EVACUATION IN BOWEL MOVEMENT

small amount hard putrid odor   breakdown of bile acids

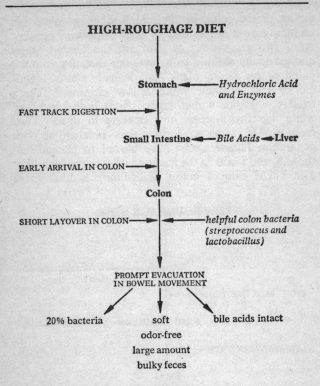

HIGH-ROUGHAGE DIET

Stomach ← *Hydrochloric Acid and Enzymes*

FAST TRACK DIGESTION →

Small Intestine ← *Bile Acids* ← Liver

EARLY ARRIVAL IN COLON →

Colon

SHORT LAYOVER IN COLON → ← *helpful colon bacteria (streptococcus and lactobacillus)*

PROMPT EVACUATION IN BOWEL MOVEMENT

20% bacteria — soft — bile acids intact

odor-free

large amount

bulky feces

among those who dwell in Japan but have made the transition to low-roughage foods.[13]

As far as cancer of the colon is concerned, it seems that more than enough of the evidence is in to implicate the modern low-fiber diet.

The following set of diagrams summarizes the situation as it now stands.

That's the bad news. But the good news is that cancer of the colon—and rectum—is a potentially *preventable* disease. And the most likely way to prevent it is simply to restore the human diet to what it should be, to what it used to be, before cancer of the large intestine killed and crippled so many victims every year. Remember, the longer we delay changing our diet the greater the chance that it will be too late. The same holds true—perhaps even in a more immediate sense—when it comes to heart attacks.

Notes

1. E. L. Wynder (1969). "Environmental Factors of Cancer of the Colon and Rectum: II. Japanese Epidemiological Data." *Cancer* 23: 1210–1220.
2. H. L. Stewart (1967). "Experimental Alimentary Tract Cancer." In *Tumors of the Alimentary Tract in Africans,* National Cancer Institute Monograph 25, Bethesda, Md., National Cancer Institute, pp. 199–217.
3. M. J. Hill (1971). "Bacteria and Aetiology of Cancer of the Large Bowel." *Lancet* 1:95–100.
4. A. Lacassagne (1961). "Carcinogenic Activity of Apcholic Acid." *Nature* 190: 1007-1008.
5. A. Haddow (1958). "Chemical Carcinogens and Their Modes of Action." *British Medical Bulletin* 14: 79–92.
6. A. Antonis (1962). "The Influence of Diet on Faecal Lipids in South African White and Bantu Prisoners." *Journal of Clinical Nutrition* 11: 142–155.
7. G. O. R. Homgren (1972). *South African Medical Journal* 46: 918.
8. J. C. Brocklehurst (1969). *Gerontologica Clinica* 2: 293.
9. H. J. Spjut (1965). "Endemic and Morphological Similarities between Spontaneous Neoplasms in Man and 3:2'Dimethyl-4-eminodiphenyl Induced Colonic Neoplasms in Rats." *Annals of Surgery* 161: 309–324.
10. R. Doll (1969). "The Geographical Distribution of Cancer." *British Journal of Cancer* 23:1–8.

11. J. C. Lawrence (1936). "Gastrointestinal Polyps. Statistical Study of Malignancy Incidence." *American Journal of Surgery* 31: 499–505.
12. G. N. Stemmermann (1970). "Patterns of Disease among Japanese Living in Hawaii." *Archives of Environmental Health* 20: 266–273.
13. See note 1 above.

4

How the Wrong Diet Can Cause a Heart Attack and Exactly How to Avoid It

The average American male over the age of forty is living on borrowed time. According to the latest medical statistics, he has one chance out of two suffering a heart attack sometime before his sixty-fifth birthday.[1] When that day comes it will probably happen like this:

One Saturday afternoon after mowing the lawn or shoveling snow off the walk, he will be slumped in his easy chair watching television and munching a snack. Without any warning he will suddenly feel a massive crushing pain just over his breastbone—"as if an elephant is sitting on his chest." He will instantly break out in a cold sweat and experience that indescribably agonizing feeling that doctors call *angor animi*—the overwhelming conviction that death is imminent. If he is lucky—and that's the scientifically accurate word—he will be rushed to the hospital in an ambulance, hooked up to a collection of shiny electronic gadgets, given oxygen, various medications, and other nonspecific treatment. A few weeks later he will leave the hospital with one-tenth to one-third of his heart muscle *totally and permanently destroyed*. That's what happens if he's *lucky*.

If he's *unlucky*, before the ambulance arrives he will slip into shock, the delicate electric circuits within the heart that control the heartbeat will be severely damaged, his heart rate will zoom to over three hundred beats a minute—and before they run the six o'clock news, *he will be dead.*

Many heart victims fall between these two extremes —some linger a few days or weeks in the hospital before slipping away. Others survive the attack but become cardiac cripples because of recurring chest pain or because not enough heart muscle has survived to efficiently pump blood through the body.

The actual figures are far from encouraging: only about 60 percent of all heart-attack victims survive the first attack (six-week survival rate), and the life expectancy of those who recover is only *five to seven years.*[1,2]

Yet the vast majority of heart attacks never have to happen. The tragedy that accounts for *one-third of all the deaths in the United States each year* is virtually unknown among millions of men and women in other parts of the world.[3,4] Sudden agonizing death or lifelong disability doesn't have to be the price of material success or the fast pace of life in modern society. The *basic* difference between those who are nearly immune to heart attacks and those 700,000 Americans who annually succumb to coronary thrombosis is basically a matter of diet. A simple, appetizing, and inexpensive addition to the deadly American diet can provide *more efficient protection from heart attacks than any other means known to medical science.*

First, consider a few simple facts about the human heart. Basically the heart is nothing more than a hollow muscle that works like a simple pump—it squeezes blood through the body by contracting and relaxing about seventy times a minute. If you take a rubber ball in your hand and squeeze it, then allow it to snap back, you will very nearly duplicate the action of your own heart.

There are some important differences however. Your hand will get tired after about a dozen squeezes, but your heart must *never* get tired. If you live to the age of seventy-five, your heart muscle will contract and relax about forty-seven million times—hopefully without missing a beat. That means 657,000 hours of nonstop functioning. Your heart can do it—it has ample capacity to spare. In those few persons who live to the age of a hundred and twenty, the heart beats *seventy-five million* times. But there is one indispensable requirement: that tough little heart muscle must have a constant and adequate supply of oxygen. The heart actually provides its own blood and oxygen requirements via the coronary arteries—a system of tiny blood vessels that circle the cardiac muscle. If, without warning, one day one of these miniature arteries that supply blood to the heart becomes obstructed, the nightmare of a heart attack becomes a sudden throbbing reality. All it takes is a tiny blood clot to clog the delicate tubing—no larger in diameter than a pencil lead. Then, as the heart muscle is deprived of life-giving oxygen, it slowly sickens and dies, setting off a vicious circle. Obstruction of the blood supply to the heart impairs the ability of that muscle to pump blood to the rest of the body and also to *itself*. As it continues to fail, it progressively reduces its own source of oxygen and fails even more rapidly.

Then the complex pacesetter buried deep in the wall of the heart muscle starts to fail and the precisely controlled muscular contractions of this marvel of engineering become irregular and haphazard. The stage is set for the ultimate catastrophe—cardiac *shock* and cardiac *death*. But even if the individual survives, heart muscle is different from any other type of muscle in the body—especially in one unfortunate way. *It does not regenerate.* Once a portion of the heart dies, it stays dead, and the burden of contracting 103,000 times a day to pump the blood has to be borne by whatever fraction of the cardiac muscles survives.

Yet heart attacks can be prevented. By combining the insights of scientists and researchers around the world, it is finally possible for potential victims to provide themselves with more protection—with less risk—than ever before possible.

Part of that protection hinges on understanding why that blood clot obstructs the tiny coronary artery in the first place. Most expert cardiologists agree that *cholesterol* is the primary cause of heart attacks. This fatty substance gradually accumulates in arteries of the human body over a period of years. It functions much like corrosion in household plumbing—clinging to the walls of the blood vessels, roughening their surfaces, and slowly narrowing their diameters. (Often the body deposits calcium into the cholesterol corrosion, adding to the problem.) Finally the tragic day comes when the tiny arteries to the heart are made so narrow by cholesterol deposits that the flow of blood begins to slow. Then a tiny clot can form, and what started out as a lazy Saturday afternoon turns into the ordeal of a lifetime.

By eliminating cholesterol from the body we should be able to eliminate all risk of heart attacks. There's only one problem—cholesterol gets into the bloodstream and the arteries in two ways. First, it is consumed in a wide variety of foods including most animal fats or animal-fat-containing substances. The list includes butter, eggs, lard, whole milk, cheese, cream, and meat. Even if it were possible to eliminate all these appetizing and nourishing items from the menu, it wouldn't affect the second source of cholesterol: the body itself. The human liver synthesizes cholesterol in impressive amounts, and there are even some experts who feel that cutting down on the cholesterol one eats forces the liver to produce more within the body. In any event, cholesterol is not harmful in itself—as a matter of fact, it is essential for the normal functioning of the human body. However, when the amount of cholesterol circulating in the blood rises above, say, 300 milligrams in each 100 milliliters of blood—known as "300 milligrams percent" or "300 mg. %"—the chances for a heart attack *increase* dramatically. Doctors have proved over and over again that reducing the cholesterol in the blood to normal levels—about 200 mg. *% or less*—substantially *reduces* the chance of a heart attack.

There are two practical ways to reduce the blood level of cholesterol. The first way is the simplest and most obvious: merely reduce the amount of fatty, cholesterol-rich foods that you eat. That involves concentrating on items which are high in what is called "unsaturated fats"—like corn oil and safflower oil—and restricting the intake of meat, eggs, cheese, and milk.

Unfortunately, abandoning the eating habits of a lifetime isn't an easy task—and to be honest, a low-fat diet involves a lot of sacrifice for the ones who eat it and the ones who cook it. The menu must be reworked to avoid or minimize eggs, bacon, butter, most cooking oils except unsaturated ones like safflower and corn oils and the like, most forms of cheese, many kinds of shellfish, whole milk, ice cream, and the kind and quantity of meat that most of us are used to eating. To further complicate the situation, the low-fat diet tends to be much more expensive than the ordinary American diet. Beyond that, virtually all convenience and commercial foods containing fat are prepared with the lowest-cost fats available, such as coconut oil or lard. These are precisely the saturated fats that must be banished from the menus of those on a low-fat anti-cholesterol diet. That puts most "instant" foods on the forbidden list and virtually eliminates commercial bakery goods such as doughnuts, cream pies, cakes with icing, custards, and puddings.

But for those who are willing to make the sacrifices —both financially and in taste appeal—there is no doubt that the low-fat diet does reduce the cholesterol level somewhat. More important, massive and costly studies of large groups of men have proven that a low-fat diet statistically reduces the chances of a heart attack. In spite of whatever advantages it may have, the standard low-fat diet is also a *low-roughage diet* with all its potential for triggering the number one form of lethal cancer, cancer of the colon and rectum.

By one of those happy coincidences that occur so rarely in the world of science, the same diet that protects against colon cancer can also effectively lower blood cholesterol and give dramatic protection from heart attacks. Consuming a diet high in cereal fiber—that is, a high-roughage diet—has been *incontrovertibly proven to increase the excretion of cholesterol from the body.* [5,6,7,8,9,10,11,12]

In fact, a high-roughage diet gives the best of both worlds. It increases the amount of cholesterol that is excreted in the daily bowel movement at the same time it reduces the amount of cholesterol secreted by the liver. [13,14]

Let's see how the process works.

A certain amount of the cholesterol normally produced by the liver is converted by the body into bile acids—the same substances described in the discussion of cancer of the colon. These bile acids ultimately find their way to the colon where they are vulnerable to destruction by the massive number of bacteria which are present. Those individuals who consume low-roughage diets—that is, most of us—harbor billions of anti-bile acid bacteria in their colons. These immediately act to break down the bile acids into two important types of substances (among others)—cancer-causing chemicals and a toxic substance called "lithocholate." [15] Lithocholate specifically acts back on the liver to cut down the conversion of cholesterol into bile acids.

That results in two unfortunate consequences. First, as less cholesterol is broken down into bile acids, cholesterol tends to accumulate in the bloodstream—*and the arteries to the heart.* Secondly, *less cholesterol finds its way into the colon*—in the form of bile acids —where it can be excreted in the feces. That is extremely critical since *the major pathway for ridding the body of hazardous and unwanted cholesterol is via the colon and the bowel movement.*[16,17] There is no doubt about this mechanism since it has been proved hundreds of times in man and experimental animals.[18]

A high-roughage diet seems to alter the type of bacteria that dominate the colon. Thus when the bile acids arrive from the liver they are *not* attacked by the friendly high-roughage-produced bacteria and are rapidly excreted in the bowel movement almost intact. That not only gets rid of significant amounts of cholesterol each day, but in a sense tricks the liver into "wasting" more and more cholesterol by converting it into bile acids that are soon eliminated.[19]

It is a beautiful, elegant, and natural way of protecting the body against one of its worst internal enemies, excessive cholesterol, and there is no doubt that it works. In a study performed in Holland, volunteers on a diet containing rolled oats—high in roughage—brought their cholesterol down from an average of 251 mg. % to 223 mg. % in only three weeks.[20] That is particularly impressive since they started at a level lower than that of most middle-aged overweight Americans. Predictably, when they resumed a conventional *low-roughage* diet, their cholesterol zoomed to its previous level within twenty-one days.

Even more amazing, high-roughage diets produce lower cholesterol levels *even though the subject may continue to eat a high-fat diet.* First observed in animals, that important finding was confirmed in a project involving two matched groups of men. One group consumed a high-fat diet plus low roughage. The other group also ate a high-fat diet but consumed an adequate amount of roughage. The high-fat, low-roughage men had cholesterol levels of 206 mg. % while the high-fat, high-roughage group had cholesterol readings of *160 mg. %*—a difference of *22 percent.* Even more convincing, those on a low-roughage diet excreted a mere *236* milligrams of bile acids a day, while those eating enough substantial fiber got rid of *305* milligrams of bile acids daily—almost *30 percent more.*[21]

To summarize, these facts seem well-documented:

1. The basic cause of heart attacks is large amounts of cholesterol circulating in the bloodstream and being deposited in the arteries of the heart.

2. A high-roughage diet reduces the absolute amount of cholesterol in the bloodstream in two ways: (a) by forcing the liver to convert cholesterol into bile salts, and subsequently, (b) increasing the amount of bile salts that are passed in the bowel movement.

There are indications that this concept has even been confirmed at the cellular level. There are substances in human blood called "triglycerides" that are important because they are reliable indicators of both the amount of cholesterol present in the bloodstream (which can be measured directly in any event) and *the amount of cholesterol being synthesized by the liver.* Those individuals who consumed a diet high in roughage showed a dramatic *decrease in blood triglycerides* in as little as five weeks, tending to indicate that restoring roughage to their diet was in fact partially *blocking the manufacture* of potentially deadly cholesterol.[22,23]

So the solution to high blood cholesterol levels —and the resulting massive death rate from heart attacks—may be a happy one. It is just possible that once they restore the roughage to their diet Americans can continue eating pretty much what they have been eating as their doctors watch their cholesterol levels descend to normal.

It seems likely that the real problem of elevated blood cholesterol—and the resultant heart attacks—

may not depend so much on the type and amount of fat which you consume. The most vital factor—and the difference between life and death for millions of Americans—may be the massive amount of cholesterol that their livers are compelled to pour out because of unending stimulation from decomposing bile acids deep within the recesses of their colons. It may well be that increasing the roughage in your diet—and thereby keeping the bile acids intact—will allow the wisdom of your own body to protect you from the needless tragedy and suffering of our society's great destroyer, the heart attack.

Notes

1. Alton Blakeslee and Jeremiah Stamler (1966). *Your Heart Has Nine Lives.* Englewood Cliffs, N.J.: Prentice-Hall, Inc. American Heart Association Condensation, p. 5.
2. *The Merck Manual of Diagnosis and Therapy.* Merck Sharp & Dohme Research Laboratories, Rahway, N.J.
3. H. C. Trowell (1960). *Non-infective Disease in Africa.* London: Edward Arnold (Publishers) Ltd.
4. V. Schire (1971). "Heart Disease in Southern Africa with Special Reference to Ischaemic Heart Disease." *South African Medical Journal* 45: 634–644.
5. M. A. Eastwood *et al.* (1973). "The Effects of Dietary Supplement of Wheat Bran and Cellulose on Faeces." *Proceedings of the Nutrition Society* 32: 22A.
6. K. S. Shurpalekar *et al.* (1971). "Effect of Inclusion of Cellulose in an 'Atherogenic' Diet on the Blood Lipids of Children." *Nature* (London) 232: 554–555.
7. A. P. de Groot *et al.* (1963). "Cholesterol-Lowering Effect of Rolled Oats." *Lancet* 2: 303–304.
8. K. S. Mathur *et al.* (1968). "Hypocholesterolaemic

Effect of Bengal Gram: A Long-term Study in Man." *British Medical Journal* 1: 30–31.

9. C. H. Edwards *et al.* (1971). "Utilization of Wheat by Adult Man: Nitrogen Metabolism, Plasma Amino Acids and Lipids." *American Journal of Clinical Nutrition* 24: 181–193.

10. R. Luyken *et al.* (1962). "The Influence of Legumes on the Serum Cholesterol Level." *Voeding* 23: 447–453.

11. A. Keys *et al.* (1960). "Diet Type (Fats Constant) and Blood Lipids in Man." *Journal of Nutrition* 70: 257–266.

12. A. Keys (1961). "Fiber and Pectin in the Diet and Serum Cholesterol Concentration in Man." *Proceedings of the Society for Experimental Biology and Medicine (New York)* 106: 555–558.

13. K. W. Heaton (1972). *Bile Salts in Health and Disease.* Edinburgh, Scotland: Churchill Livingstone.

14. Editorial, *New England Journal of Medicine,* July 9, 1970.

15. M. J. Hill *et al.* (1971). "Bacteria and Aetiology of Cancer of the Large Bowel." *Lancet* 1: 95–100.

16. H. C. Trowell (1972). "Ischaemic Heart Disease and Dietary Fiber." *American Journal of Clinical Nutrition* 25: 926–932.

17. H. C. Trowell (1972). "Fiber: A Natural Hypocholesteroemic Agent." *American Journal of Clinical Nutrition* 25: 464–465.

18. B. E. Gustafsson (1969). "Influence of the Diet on the Turnover of Bile Acids in Germ-Free and Conventional Rats." *British Journal of Nutrition* 23: 429–442.

19. A. Antonis *et al.* (1962). "The Influence of Diet on Fecal Lipids in South African White and Bantu Prisoners." *American Journal of Clinical Nutrition* 11: 142–155.

20. See note 7 above.

21. See note 8 above.

22. K. W. Heaton *et al.* (1970). "Comparison of Two Bile Acid Binding Agents, Cholestyramine and Lignin." In *Advance Abstracts of the Fourth World Congress on Gastroenterology,* p. 447.
23. K. W. Heaton *et al.* (1971). "An In Vivo Comparison of Two Bile Salt Binding Agents, Cholestyramine and Lignin." *Scandinavian Journal of Gastroenterology* 6: 281–286.

5

Diverticulosis and Appendicitis: The Treatment Can Make You Sicker

Diverticulosis is the single most common disease of the colon. Approximately 40 percent of all Americans over the age of forty are its victims and almost 70 percent of those past seventy years old suffer from the disease.[1,2] It has reached endemic proportions in North America and Europe and causes untold suffering and disability.

The most astounding aspect of the condition is that as recently as 1916 it was not even mentioned in medical textbooks! [3] Like some strange new island arising from the depths of the ocean, diverticulosis has suddenly appeared to blight the lives of millions. Although as recently as 1960 official medical opinion held that diverticulosis was a "symptomless disease," a "silent benign condition,"[4] it is now well-established as a cause of the following collection of symptoms: [5]

1. Nausea

2. Heartburn

3. Excessive gas

4. Bloating and distention

5. Severe abdominal pain

6. Rectal tenderness

7. Incomplete emptying of the rectum

8. Constipation

No one knows exactly how many millions of Americans suffer from diverticulosis because many cases are never diagnosed while the patient is still alive.[6] The victims waste tens of millions of dollars each year on antacid pills, powders, and liquids which generally provide little relief of the symptoms and allow the disease to progress.

Unfortunately, that's the least of it. Almost two out of every ten cases of diverticulosis progress to *diverticulitis,* a dangerous and potentially fatal disease that can involve constant pain, chills, fever, bleeding, and perforation of the intestine.[7]

Let's take a moment to look at the design and function of the colon so that we can understand exactly what diverticulosis and diverticulitis are, what causes them, and how they can be prevented or cured.

The human large intestine, or colon, can be compared to a long string of very short link sausages. At the point where each sausage is joined together at the end, the colon has a circular band of muscle which can expand and contract. In effect, these muscular bands function as valves at the end of each segment, opening and closing in perfect synchronization to move the intestinal contents forward on their way out of the body. As one end of a segment opens, the other end closes, the muscles contract and the feces move ahead. The effect is like that of a digestive conveyor belt pushing the semiliquid feces forward progressively. If all goes well, the feces are hustled out of the body in short order. Success in this conveying project depends on three factors: [8]

1. Maintaining the diameter of the colon as

wide as possible—the larger the pipe, the faster the flow.

2. Assuring that the contents are liquid or at least semiliquid to avoid allowing too much water to be absorbed from the feces and drying the fecal mass.

3. Being sure to empty the fecal contents promptly when the urge arises to prevent further drying and hardening.

But if all doesn't go well, things turn out quite differently. If the products of digestion drift lazily through the colon, as the months and years go by the diameter of the colon shrinks down. That obviously lengthens transport time, since a one-inch pipe cannot provide the flow that a four-inch pipe can. Meanwhile, water is continuously being absorbed from the fecal material, which becomes progressively harder and drier. These factors cause a critical increase in the internal pressure in the colon—and that's where big problems start. The wall of the colon isn't very strong to begin with, and at its weakest points it begins to bulge out in a series of blisters like tiny rubber balloons. Once the thin stretchy wall of the colon pops out in these bubbles, *it never goes back to normal.* Instead of a large-bore smooth-walled colon, the victim of diverticulosis is left with a narrow pipe that has many pockets and bulges along its length. Digestion is profoundly disturbed and the eight major symptoms of diverticular disease may suddenly become prominent. The diagnosis is easily made by taking an X-ray of the large intestine—one or dozens of the little pouches are clearly seen protruding from the sides of the colon.[9]

Sometimes a small piece of hardened fecal matter can plug up the narrow neck of these balloons (or "diverticula," as they are known)—or the opening that connects the pouch with the colon can become obstructed on its own. Then inflammation, infection, and abscess formation can occur. When that happens, *diverticulosis* gives way to *diverticulitis*—the *-itis* ending on the word signifying that infection of the little balloons is the problem. Severe pain, massive bleeding, and even death can occur as a result.[10]

From about 1920—when diverticulosis and diverticulitis were first recognized as distinct diseases—until recently, the treatment was, to say the least, unexciting. The usual therapy for diverticulosis was mineral oil as a laxative to combat the stubborn constipation and a *low-roughage diet,* supposedly to "rest" the colon.[11] In some cases, even surgery was performed. For diverticulitis, the treatment was morphine for pain, antibiotics and rest for the infection, and for severe cases *surgical removal* of the affected part of the intestine.

The patients weren't satisfied because their suffering usually went on unabated. The physicians weren't satisfied because they were neither able to understand nor effectively treat the most widely encountered disease of the colon.

Then, fortunately for all of us, the same group of British (and later American) physicians and surgeons who pioneered in the discovery of high-roughage diets as the prevention of colon cancer, heart attacks, and other conditions turned their attention to diverticulosis and diverticulitis. Even in the early stages of their investigation they were struck by some fascinating findings. First, they observed that diverticulosis (and diverticulitis) were extremely rare in Africa, Korea, Singapore, Malaysia, Iran, India, New Guinea and other areas depending on a high-roughage diet.[12,13,14] Conversely, the diseases were very common in areas of low-roughage consumption such as the United States and Britain. Predictably, the incidence was intermediate in countries where the diet was in transition from high roughage to low

CHICK PEAS

By Kavita Mariwalla
Kidsday Staff Reporter

13 ounces chick peas
1 large onion, chopped fine
2 tablespoons vegetable oil
½ teaspoon chili powder
½ teaspoon cumin seeds
½ teaspoon coriander seeds
salt and pepper to taste
½ teaspoon fresh grated ginger
¼ teaspoon tumeric
1½ tablespoons crushed tomatoes
1 teaspoon lemon juice

Grind ⅓ of the chick peas. Set aside. Fry onion in vegetable oil until golden brown. Add next 6 ingredients. Add ground chick peas and unground chick peas to mixture. Add crushed tomatoes and simmer 15 minutes. Add lemon juice. Serve with pita bread.

```
D P W B J H F D B E U B G T D
X S H X Y G T B P B G S D P S
Y A D L A I R O M E M U N K P
M M N P O A Z P O N M N L J K
S Q H I A C B D L F E G H I W
E F J L L N P Q C D F H B A A
V L L O G N I M M I W S O U R
I N C O D B H G D P T T G S M
T S L P W U V R A Z Q R F T S
A C K B D E S Y K M O O I U E
L C D A G H R R A W M H U P L
E H W A B Z Q S R W L S K M A
R E S U M M E R S Y B D F G S
```

Find these words: Memorial Day, pool, summer, sun, shorts, swimming, warm, flowers, sales, relatives roughage.[15] Further evidence came from the fact that during World War II the incidence of diverticulosis actually *decreased* in Britain when the only available bread had a much higher roughage content —and, incidentally, where ultra-refined carbohydrates like sugar were in very short supply.[16] Elsewhere in the world the researchers discovered that those who were in the process of switching from a high-roughage diet to a low-roughage diet faced mounting affliction with diverticular disease. That included the Hawaiian and Californian Japanese, the American blacks, and citified Africans.[17] Additional confirmation of the role that low-roughage diets played in diverticulosis came from the fact that those who succumbed to the other diseases of low-roughage diet intake—such as heart attacks, appendicitis, hemorrhoids, and cancer of the colon—also had a higher-than-average incidence of diverticular disease.[18] Even rats maintained on a low-roughage diet came down with diverticulosis.

The next step was a bold one. A few intrepid physicians abandoned the traditional *low-roughage* diet and deliberately fed *high-roughage* diets to diverticulosis-stricken patients. At that time, they came under sharp criticism. They were accused of irritating the already hyper-irritable intestine by forcing it to deal with the seeds, strings, and skins contained in vegetables and even larger amounts of cereal fiber. But the results proved the doctors right.

In one pioneer study carried out in England, seventy patients who had received little benefit from the traditional low-roughage treatment were exposed to the high-roughage diet. *Sixty-two of them obtained dramatic relief with this therapy.* That translates into a relief rate of about *88 percent*—without drugs, without surgery, and without risk. Nearly all of them were able to discontinue their previous medications and lead a normal life.[19]

The same kind of results were obtained over and over again in subsequent groups of patients until, at

the present time, more and more physicians are selecting a high-roughage diet as *the standard treatment* for
diverticulosis. Interestingly enough, once it absorbs
water and is processed by the digestive system, "roughage" quickly becomes "softage" and rapidly restores
the *functions* to normal. Regrettably no amount of
dietary alteration can restore the *structure* of the
ballooned-out portions of the colon to normal, although as long as patients remain on their high-fiber
diet, they are remarkably free of symptoms.

There is one vitally important lesson to be learned
from the experience with diverticulosis. Since the
disease apparently takes about forty years or so to
damage the intestinal wall, the ideal time to begin
avoiding the irreversible damage is during childhood.
A child who is raised on the typical American high-
sugar, ultra-refined carbohydrate, low-roughage diet
has every chance of developing serious diverticular
disease—not to mention cancer of the colon, heart
attacks, and all the rest.

The major offenders in the average child's diet are:

1. White bread

2. Low-roughage sugar-strewn breakfast cereals

3. High-sugar soft drinks

4. Hamburgers, pizzas, hot dogs, ice cream, and
dessert products aimed specifically at children.

Ironically the same manufacturers can produce high-
quality high-roughage products with a better taste and
greater nutritional value. To make matters worse,
some cereal manufacturers actually make high-roughage products but deliberately do not promote them
to children or parents. Most of these high-fiber "all
bran" type cereals are aimed at older folks where
much of the damage has already been done.

Another consequence of the traditional low-roughage diet is particularly unfortunate for youngsters and people under forty. That's the problem of appendicitis. Most of us consider inflammation of the appendix a relatively minor matter in comparison with cancer and heart disease. In the United States, however, appendicitis is the *number one abdominal emergency* —surgeons perform approximately *two hundred thousand appendectomies* each year. At an average charge of $350 for the surgery and anesthesia, $450 for the hospital, and $200 in lost wages, that adds up to the colossal cost of *two hundred million dollars each year.* Much more tragic, there are about 20,000 deaths annually from appendicitis or its complications.[20] That is intolerable—especially from a condition that is probably preventable and need never have happened in the first place. A brief survey of appendicitis brings the entire picture quickly into focus.

The full medical name of that little troublemaker is the "vermiform appendix"—that means "the worm-like tubing that hangs down." That's a pretty good description of the diminutive organ. About two and a half inches long, more or less the diameter of your little finger, the appendix is a short length of dead-end hollow tubing that leads off from the point where the small intestine goes into the large intestine. Anatomically, it usually lies just underneath a point several inches to the right and below your belt buckle. Its purpose has long since been forgotten—the appendix may be the remnant of a now-extinct extra length of intestinal tubing. But one thing is certain—it is potentially dangerous. When appendicitis occurs, this is how it can happen:

At any hour of the day or night, without any warning whatsoever, the appendix swells and becomes inflamed. The tiny opening to the rest of the intestine is swiftly sealed, the little appendix fills with fluid, becomes hot and red, and unless surgery is performed *immediately,* it may rupture. When that happens, liquid feces are sprayed all over the abdominal cavity, resulting in potentially fatal peritonitis. One of the worst features of acute appendicitis is that it can happen anywhere and anytime. It is a death-dealing possibility in a spaceship on the way to the moon, in a submarine on the bottom of the ocean, in the Amazon jungle, and in the desolation of Antarctica. Less dramatically but more commonly, it can threaten mother and child during the course of a pregnancy.

A careful survey of incidence and extent of appendicitis reveals the same fascinating progression as the other low-roughage disease—colon cancer, heart attacks, and all the rest. Before about 1880 appendicitis was a rare condition.[21] Then slowly it began to crop up in Britain and the United States. About 1920 a distinguished English physician made the astute observation that appendicitis was frequent in affluent schoolboys who attended posh private schools and dined on low-fiber white bread, cakes, and pastry. It was much rarer in "unfortunate" orphans who subsisted on the cheap, coarse, high-fiber bread offered by the orphanage.[22] Later, investigators turned their attention to the underdeveloped countries and found a by now familiar pattern. Appendicitis was virtually unknown among those who followed the native high-roughage diet. In one section of Africa, less than *3 percent* of the abdominal surgery performed on *Africans* was for appendicitis. In the same area, more than *30 percent* of the abdominal surgery performed on Europeans was for appendicitis.[23] The major difference between the two groups was the amount of roughage in their respective diets.

In nation after nation appendicitis was found to be a rare disease. In Kenya, Uganda, the Sudan, Ghana, Nigeria, Rhodesia, South Africa, Rumania, Egypt, and India, those on high-roughage diets hardly had to worry about inflammation of the appendix.[24,25,26] Those foreigners on low-roughage diets had the usual Western incidence of the disease. In the process of the research there were some ingenious observations. For example, black African stevedores who worked unloading ships in the harbor seemed to have a higher rate of appendicitis than other members of their families. This apparent contradiction was finally explained when observers noted that the stevedores were fed Western low-roughage fare from the ships they were unloading. Similarly, Sudanese soldiers who served in the British Army during World War II and Congolese students in Belgium all showed much higher rates of appendicitis than their relatives back home. The relation of diet to infections of the appendix was reaffirmed as the rate of appendicitis dropped in Switzerland during World War II when the Swiss ate less refined bread, more vegetables, and cut their consumption of refined carbohydrates such as sugar.[27]

The exact mechanism that causes appendicitis is unclear, but it might well be this: Under the influence of a low-roughage diet, the entire digestive system goes into slow motion. The food dawdles on its way through the intestine, and as each hour passes, more and more of the water is absorbed. This encourages the formation of "fecaliths"—tiny, rock-hard pebbles of fecal material. As the fecal stream flows slowly through the intestines, one of these small concretions may drop into the opening to the appendix and seal it off. Sometimes the stagnant intestine simply allows bacteria to multiply and the resulting inflammation closes off the appendicial opening. The pressure within the appendix increases, stretching its already thin wall and making it vulnerable to the everpresent bacteria. Infection and inflammation soon follow and another red-hot appendix cries out for the surgeon's knife.

It does not seem to be a coincidence that those individuals who have had appendicitis also have an increased tendency to later develop cancer of the colon.[28] It is probably another unfortunate legacy of the low-roughage diet.

As far as appendicitis is concerned, the chain of evidence is unbroken. Based on studies on the clinical course and medical records of millions of cases in over twenty countries during the past fifty years, it appears that appendicitis is a preventable disease. The $200,000,000 stolen from our national economy each year and the 20,000 lives wasted can probably be saved. All we have to do is restore the roughage to our diet—the same roughage that was there since the days of the cave men—until we took it out.

Notes

1. T. G. Parks (1968). "Post-Mortem Studies on the Colon with Special Reference to Diverticular Disease." *Proceedings of the Royal Society of Medicine* 61: 932.
2. L. E. Hughes (1969). "Post Mortem Survey of Diverticular Disease of the Colon." *Gut* 10: 336–351.
3. W. H. M. Telling *et al.* (1917). *British Journal of Surgery* 4: 468.
4. R. L. Cecil and R. F. Loeb (1955). *Textbook of Medicine.* Philadelphia: W. B. Saunders & Co., p. 886.
5. N. S. Painter *et al.* (1972). "Unprocessed Bran in Treatment of Diverticular Disease of the Colon." *British Medical Journal* 2: 137–140.
6. N. S. Painter *et al.* (1971). "Diverticular Disease of the Colon." *British Medical Journal* 2: 450–454.
7. C. G. Schowengerdt *et al.* (1969). "Diverticulosis, Diverticulitis, and Diabetes: A Review of 740 Cases." *Archives of Surgery* 98: 500–504.
8. N. S. Painter *et al.* (1965). "Segmentation and the Localization of Intraluminal Pressures in the Human Colon." *Gastroenterology* 49: 169–177.
9. S. Arfdwidsson (1964). "Pathogenesis of Multiple Diverticula of the Sigmoid Colon in Diverticular Disease." *Acta Chirurgica Scandinavica* Supplement 342.
10. F. C. Fleischner *et al.* (1965). "Revised Concepts on Diverticular Disease of the Colon II." *Radiology* 84: 599–609.

11. P. W. Brown *et al.* (1937). "Prognosis of Diverticulitis and Diverticulosis of the Colon." *Journal of the American Medical Association* 109: 1328–1333.
12. K. J. Keeley (1958). *Medical Proceeding* 4: 281.
13. E. H. Kim (1964). "Hiatus Hernia and Diverticulum of the Colon." *New England Journal of Medicine* 271: 764–768.
14. J. Kyle *et al.* (1967). "Incidence of Diverticulitis." *Scandinavian Journal of Gastroenterology* 2: 77–80.
15. G. N. Stemmermann (1970). "Patterns of Disease among Japanese Living in Hawaii." *Archives of Environmental Health* 20: 266–273.
16. T. L. Cleave *et al.* (1969). *Diabetes, Coronary Thrombosis, and the Saccharine Diseases,* 2nd ed. Bristol: Wright.
17. E. J. Kocour (1937). "Diverticulosis of the Colon." *American Journal of Surgery* 37: 433–436.
18. See note 5 above.
19. See note 5 above.
20. D. P. Burkitt (1971). "The Aetiology of Appendicitis." *British Journal of Surgery* 58: 695–699.
21. F. Treves (1902). *Allbutt's System of Medicine.* T. C. Allbutt, ed. New York: Macmillan Co., Publishers, p. 3.
22. A. Rendle Short (1920). "The Causation of Appendicitis." *British Journal of Surgery* 8: 171–188.
23. J. R. M. Miller (1955). *East African Medical Journal* 32: 219.
24. F. W. Vint (1937). *East African Medical Journal* 113: 332.
25. E. A. Badoe (1967). *Ghana Medical Journal* 6: 69.
26. P. Omo-Dare *et al.* (1966). *West African Medical Journal* 15: 217.
27. A. Fleish (1946). *Schweizerische medizinische wochenschrift* 37/38: 889.
28. D. P. Burkitt (1970). "Relationship as a Clue to Causation." *Lancet* 2: 1237–1240.

6

Constipation, Hemorrhoids, Varicose Veins, and Deadly Phlebitis— Four Accidents That Never Had to Happen

Constipation has the dual distinction of simultaneously being the most common and the most neglected affliction of modern times. In Western countries, nearly 100 percent of the population suffers from the condition at one time or another. Yet no one except the victims seems to take it seriously. Even the most prestigious medical works underestimate the importance of the malfunction: "The physician must patiently explain that daily bowel movements are not essential, that no real harm comes from the bowel not moving for up to four days." This text continues: "A real ill often develops . . . based on the fatuous conviction that the body must rid itself of fecal residues in a stereotyped way and very frequently."[1]

On the other hand, almost everyone *instinctively* feels that their body functions best if they *do* have a regular, well-formed daily bowel movement without straining. Recently more and more evidence has accumulated to suggest that instinct is correct. Careful observations of groups in underdeveloped countries consuming unprocessed diets show that normal bowel patterns consist of daily movements.[2]

Regular bowel function seems rational from another point of view—we consume food daily, we digest food daily, and we should be able to eliminate residues of digestion daily. The human colon is not a stainless-steel holding tank; it is a living part of an organism which is continually absorbing a wide variety of potent chemicals from the feces it contains. The longer the feces remain putrefying in the colon, the greater the chance that serious consequences will occur. (As we have seen, cancer is a real danger,[8] and the chemicals produced in stagnant feces tend to increase blood cholesterol.[4]) Constipation, the production of dry hard stools at less than daily intervals, keeps the hazardous substances in the feces in intimate contact with the intestinal wall far longer than necessary. A man weighing one hundred eighty pounds who consumes a low-roughage diet might pass about one-quarter pound of feces daily. At that rate, it will take him about two years for his bowel movements to equal his body weight. By comparison, the same man on a high-roughage diet might have a half-pound bowel movement daily and excrete his total body weight in a single year. That extra forty-four pounds of fecal residue which lies stagnant in his body for up to twelve months certainly can't do him any good.

If scientific medicine doesn't take constipation seriously, there are dozens of drug companies who do. They turn out a dazzling variety of powders, pills, liquids, and even candy and chewing gum, to do for people what they can't do for themselves. In the United States alone, the laxative industry garners millions and millions of dollars each year—and the products it purveys range all the way from harmless to hazardous. For example, mineral oil, a popular home laxative, can interfere with the absorption of vitamin A. And excessive use of certain laxatives has been shown to totally destroy the nerve network of portions of the colon.[5] Continuous use of any laxative drug, of course, can interfere with the normal functioning of the digestive system and produce problems, including a dependence on laxatives. Just as important, most of the money spent on laxative preparations is money wasted. *Constipation is virtually impossible on a diet that contains adequate roughage.* The same two cents a day that buys protection from so many serious diseases also purchases freedom from constipation.

This is the way the process works: Dietary fiber is made up of three basic compounds—lignin, cellulose, and hemi-cellulose. If there is enough fiber in the diet these substances work in unison on the intestines to produce regular, easy-to-pass bowel movements.[6]

The precise action of the three components of fiber *against* constipation as delineated by some researchers is a fascinating one. As the bacteria in the colon act on dietary fiber, one of the by-products they produce is a group of "fatty acids." These substances—which go by names like acetic, butyric, and propionic acid— are natural laxatives, and on a high-roughage diet they assure regular evacuation of the fast-moving fecal contents.[7]

At the same time one of the three components of roughage, *lignin,* seems to balance the laxative effects of dietary fiber and prevent runaway diarrhea.[8]

Roughage also works against constipation in two other ways. First, it increases the bulk of the bowel movement so that the fecal contents stimulate muscular action of the bowel and push their way through. Part of this is explained by the ability of each gram of fiber to increase the volume of the stool up to twenty times. Fiber also absorbs substantial amounts of water and may soak up additional liquid compounds from the small intestine.

The precise method of using roughage to overcome constipation is simple and straightforward. *High-Roughage Diet Plan Number Three* (see Chapter 7) *should provide prompt and permanent relief in nearly every case*. In one research project in Britain, nearly every patient was cured of constipation in short order by adding about half an ounce (fifteen grams) of bran to his daily diet. To make the daily roughage replacement even more appetizing—and incidentally more portable for those who must travel or eat in restaurants—another British team suggested a type of cracker which incorporates the total twenty-four-hour roughage requirement in a simple and appetizing form.[9]

These crackers have been adapted to American tastes and the recipe appears in Chapter 10 under the name "Hi-Fiber Crackers." Each of these tiny, crisp onion, cheese, or garlic-flavored crackers contains about three grams of unprocessed bran; five of them provide the daily requirement of roughage for the *average* person. (Although they are not yet available in the United States, they are easy enough to make at home until commercial production begins.)

One of the most common—and least popular—side effects of constipation is hemorrhoids. Nearly half of the entire nation over the age of fifty suffers from hemorrhoids—or as they are popularly known, "piles."[10]

Actually a hemorrhoid is nothing more than a big bulging vein which lies near the surface of the skin or the mucous membrane in the area of the anus. There are two types of hemorrhoids: internal and external. The external ones are visible to the patient —with the aid of a mirror—and consist of little purplish lumps or tags around the anal opening that become swollen when the individual strains at a bowel movement. Sometimes blood clots form within the distended veins and the hemorrhoids then become tender and painful. The thin layer of skin over each hemorrhoid may even become ulcerated and bleed with every defecation.

Internal hemorrhoids, on the other hand, are rarely seen by the sufferer since they affect veins higher up in the anal canal. These veins are more extensive than the external ones and can cause considerable bleeding. Although the amount of blood lost from hemorrhoids is rarely substantial, the bleeding itself can lead to other hazards. Since cancer of the colon and rectum can *also* cause bleeding, more than one person with rectal bleeding has brushed it off as "just my hemorrhoids acting up again," neglected to see his doctor, and allowed his colon cancer to grow past the point where it could be treated successfully.

Hemorrhoids are a major cause of pain and disability in every industrialized country on a low-roughage diet. In addition, the economic consequences from lost wages and lowered production can scarcely be calculated. The most effective treatment for hemorrhoids up until now has been surgery—relatively painful, expensive, and time-consuming. Furthermore because hemorrhoids affect the anal area and touch the "toilet taboo" of Americans, most victims suffer in silence while spending tens of millions of dollars yearly on "preparations" and suppositories which *cannot possibly affect the basic problem.*

As a matter of fact, until recently, physicians were at a loss to explain exactly what caused hemorrhoids. The standard statement went something like: ". . . presumably result from conditions that produce rectal venous congestion such as constipation, pregnancy, rectal disease, diarrhea, and portal hypertension."[11] That is hardly a definitive explanation.

As nutritional researchers around the world turned their attention to the problems of constipation, they encountered some puzzling questions. Why should constipation make the suffering of those with hemorrhoids so intense? Why should it be so out of proportion to the mechanical pressure of the hardened fecal matter pressing against the swollen veins? They carefully retraced the route of venous drainage and made some interesting discoveries.

The purpose of the veins of the circulatory system is simply to return the blood from outlying parts of the body to the heart. The smaller veins of the anus and rectum empty into the larger veins of the pelvis just as smaller rivers drain into larger ones. On a low-roughage diet, the investigators reasoned, the dry, hardened feces that collect day after day in the colon push outward and compress the large veins nearby. This pressure acts like a dam, prevents the blood from draining out of the anal and rectal veins, and causes tremendous return pressure. The result is the swollen, inflamed, knotted veins that we call hemorrhoids.[12]

Other investigators agreed with this finding in principle but felt there might be still another important factor causing hemorrhoids. They noted that those on low-roughage diets tend to strain and struggle to pass their small hardened stools, and in the process of straining, the pressure *within the major veins* can rise to amazing levels. For example, the pressure inside the vena cava has been measured at 300 to 400 millimeters of mercury, or about 250 to 350 percent greater than normal systolic blood pressure![13] This pressure is directly transmitted to the rectal and anal veins and can in itself balloon them out, weaken their walls, and result in permanent hemorrhoids.

The scientists also noted that hemorrhoids—internal or external—were rare in Africans and Asians on a traditional high-roughage diet. Obviously there is never any hard, dry fecal material to distend their colons, press on their veins, and cause the destructive return pressure. In addition, Africans and Asians never have to strain while moving their bowels. But as soon as they begin to adopt the Western low-fiber diet, they almost invariably begin to show signs of hemorrhoids.

Clearly there is no way to reverse the damage already done to the veins of the rectum and anus. But a high-roughage diet can help prevent bleeding, relieve the pressure within the stretched and distorted veins, and help forestall the formation of *new* hemorrhoids. It can also provide freedom from the expensive ritual of ointments, suppositories, laxatives, and all the rest of the patent medicines that hemorrhoid sufferers turn to in desperation.

Another complaint of modern life may have the same basic cause as hemorrhoids. About 10 percent of the entire population of the United States—that is, 22 million people—suffer from varicose veins. These distended veins of the legs, in addition to being annoying and unsightly, can cause swelling, muscle cramps, tension, and soreness. Occasionally they can result in open oozing and skin ulcers. But beyond that, they can even lead to potentially fatal consequences.

Let's see how the distention occurs:

Ever since man has walked on his hind legs, the body has had a difficult assignment in getting blood back to the heart from the lowest portions of the anatomy. The blood supplying the lower legs and feet is brought upward by an ingenious mechanism known as the "muscle pump." With each step the powerful muscles of the legs squeeze blood upward in the deep veins of each lower limb. But there's a catch. Each time the blood rises in the veins it tends to fall back down again. However, built into each vein is a system of valves—like locks in a canal—and every time blood is forced upward by the muscles, it is kept at that level by these valves. If these valves are somehow destroyed, the blood cannot rise effectively, it stagnates, and all the annoying and disabling symptoms of varicose veins appear.

The treatment of mild varicose veins is nonmedical —elastic stockings or support hose are generally used. But to an attractive—and still young—man or woman, elastic stockings are hardly the most appealing fashion accessory. The ultimate cure for varicose veins is still surgery—stripping out those veins with broken valves or tying off the affected veins high up on the legs.

Until recently, varicose veins have been blamed on such vague causes as standing for long periods of time. But among those people on a high-roughage diet, less than *one-tenth of one percent* suffer from varicosities of the veins[14]—although nearly 100 percent of *them* are on their feet for long periods.

A far more likely explanation for varicose veins is the same combination of factors that cause hemorrhoids—since hemorrhoids are actually nothing more than varicose veins of the rectum and anus. Although a high-fiber diet may take the pressure off the large veins of the pelvis and abdomen and unblock the drainage system—thus helping the circulation of blood in the veins of the legs—there is no way that it can make the stretched and swollen veins deep within the legs go back to normal. However, restoring roughage to the diet can prevent further damage from occurring, and most important of all, it may reduce the chances of the most awesome complications of varicose veins —phlebothrombosis, thrombophlebitis, and pulmonary embolism.

Let's take the first term. "Phlebothrombosis" comes from two Greek words: *phlebo,* meaning "vein," and *thrombo,* meaning "clot." Therefore *phlebothrombosis* means a blood clot in a vein—and that *is* a problem. As the blood begins to sludge and stagnate in the damaged deep veins of the legs, a blood clot may form. At first it is no more than a tiny blob of jellylike material poised in the blood vessel. But gradually it may acquire a "tail" stretching out behind it for some distance, and it may even become attached to the wall of the vein. Then the vein itself can become inflamed. At that point, the condition is known as "thrombophlebitis," or simply "phlebitis"—the *-itis* ending, as usual, indicates an inflammatory process is underway. Severe pain, swelling, and tenderness often occur at that point—but the worst is yet to come. Without any warning the clot can suddenly break loose and race swiftly upward through progressively larger veins until it reaches the lungs, where it causes a dreaded "pulmonary embolism."

While the clot is stationary it is known as a "thrombus," but once it begins its deadly journey it becomes known as an "embolism" from the Greek word for "plug." And that's exactly what it does.

That mobile clot may plug the pulmonary arteries, resulting in circulatory collapse, heart failure, and death.

Unfortunately there is no way of predicting in advance when or even *if* a clot will break loose, become an embolus, and shoot upward into the lungs. That's one reason that a case of thromboembolism can be described as a "loaded shotgun aimed toward the lungs," ready to discharge dozens of blood clots into the vulnerable respiratory system.

The accepted treatment for thrombophlebitis is anticoagulants and perhaps surgically tying off the large veins toward the upper part of the leg to isolate the clots from the vital organs. However, everyone involved would agree that prevention is a far better approach. The best-known prevention—to date—consists of trying to *prevent the underlying disease.* The only known way to accomplish that is to normalize the operation of the digestive system by restoring the absent and essential roughage to the diet. That should, if the experts are right, relieve the obstruction of the large pelvic and abdominal veins and lower the pressure within the abdomen at the time of defecation, thereby preventing the stagnation of blood flow that predisposes toward clot formation.

Although nobody dies of constipation or hemorrhoids or varicose veins, they are still annoying and disabling diseases afflicting untold millions of men and women—with the small but real hazard of pulmonary embolism and its potentially fatal barrage of blood clots to the lungs.

For years these conditions were dismissed as the "penalties of civilization," but it is rapidly becoming apparent that consuming the so-called civilized diet is one of the *least* civilized things that we do. Tens of millions of Africans and Asians live their entire lives without the burdens of these diseases—and if we go back to the diet that we never should have left, so can we.

Notes

1. *Merck Manual of Diagnois and Therapy.*
2. A. R. P. Walker (1969). "Bowel Transit Times in Bantu Population." *British Medical Journal* 3: 238. A. R. P. Walker (1961). "Crude Fiber, Bowel Motility, and Pattern of Diet." *South African Medical Journal* 35: 114–115.
3. A. Laccassagne (1961). "Carcinogenic Activity of Apcholic Acid." *Nature* 190: 1007–1008.
4. K. W. Heaton (1972). *Bile Salts in Health and Disease.* Edinburgh, Scotland: Churchill Livingstone.
5. N. S. Painter (1972). "Unprocessed Bran in Treatment of Diverticular Disease of the Colon." *British Medical Journal* 1: 137–140.
6. D. A. T. Southgate (1969). "Determination of Carbohydrates in Food. II. Unavailable Carbohydrates." *Journal of Scientific Food Agriculture* 20: 331–335.
7. R. D. Williams (1936). "The Effect of Cellulose, Hemi-Cellulose, and Lignin on the Weight of the Stool." *Journal of Nutrition* 11: 443–449.
8. K. W. Heaton (1970). "Comparison of Two Bile Acid Binding Agents, Cholestyramine and Lignin." *Advance Abstracts of the Fourth World Congress on Gastroenterology.*
9. P. F. Plumly (November 1973). "Dietary Management of Diverticular Disease." *Journal of the American Dietetic Association* 63(5).
10. D. P. Burkitt (1972). "Varicose Veins, Deep Vein Thrombosis, and Haemorrhoids." *British Medical Journal* 2: 556–561.
11. *Merck Manual of Diagnosis and Therapy.*
12. T. L. Cleave (1969). *Diabetes, Coronary Thrombosis, and the Saccharine Diseases*, 2nd ed. Bristol: John

Wright and Sons, Ltd. T. L. Cleave (1959). "Varicose Veins. Nature's Error or Man's?" *Lancet* 2: 172–175.

13. E. P. Sharpey-Schafer, cited by P. Shemilt, *British Journal of Surgery* 4: 695.

14. See note 10.

7

Two Cents a Day to Keep the Doctor Away— The Key to Survival We All Throw Away

Based on the judgments of five hundred prominent medical authorities as expressed in over six hundred medical articles and books published around the world (for an indication of the research, see the Selected Bibliography), there seems little doubt that dietary fiber or roughage is an essential part of the human diet. To exist on a "modern" low-roughage diet is to court premature death and disability. Lack of roughage in our diet is a deficiency—just as lack of protein or minerals is a deficiency. For a long and happy life that roughage deficiency must be corrected.

There are several ways of restoring adequate dietary fiber to our daily diets. First, we might switch to the staple menu of rural Africans and Asians. That means ground corn, boiled bananas, freshly dug potatoes, and plenty of beans. Most Americans would be understandably reluctant to make that kind of substitution.

The second possibility is to try and regulate our diets by selecting only those foods with the highest roughage content from the grocer's shelves. That's a very difficult assignment—for a couple of reasons. Over 90 percent of the 11,000 items stocked by the average supermarket have had nearly every scrap of roughage removed in the refining or manufacturing process.

Look at some examples:

1. "Instant" potatoes, "instant" rice, cake mixes, puddings, desserts, gravies, stuffings, cereals, and the like have been stripped of dietary fiber.

2. Bread, pastry, commercial baked goods, and "convenience" items containing ultra-refined flour are nearly all uniformly low in dietary fiber.

To convert the average American diet to a high-roughage diet would require the following changes:

1. Use only whole-grain products such as whole wheat, rolled oats, and brown rice.

2. Consume *fresh* fruits and vegetables raw or barely cooked with seeds, strings, and skins intact, if at all possible.

3. Cut to a bare minimum consumption of refined sugar, soft drinks, fats, and meat.

Ninety-nine percent of American families will reject that regimen since they have been conditioned to the "fashionable" and seductive low-roughage routine. Beyond that, there is an important element of reality. With food prices already sky-high, few individuals or families can afford the approximately 30 percent additional cost of converting their daily fare to the ideal high-roughage diet. But that doesn't mean they have to suffer the agonies of heart attacks or colon cancer or all the rest of the roughage-deficiency diseases. There is an easy and appetizing way out.

Look at the situation this way. Our goal is to fortify the diet by bringing the roughage level up to about twenty-four grams each day. Since our diet contains approximately six grams of dietary fiber already, there is a daily deficit of about eighteen grams of roughage, or just a little over half an ounce. What we need is a palatable, wholesome, and inexpensive source of dietary fiber. We need something that can be added to our daily diet almost as easily as a vitamin pill to bring our roughage consumption right up to normal. Many such products have been tested, and the one that seems to fit the requirement best of all is a natural part of each grain of wheat that is usually discarded in the milling process or used as animal fodder. It is called "bran," and it makes up the first six layers of outer coating of the wheat berry.

Bran is cheap—running about sixty cents a pound. That's roughly a month's supply, which works out to about two cents a day. As a source of roughage, bran is outstanding—it is 12 percent dietary fiber and is five times as effective in restoring roughage to the body as whole-wheat flour. That means a small amount added to the daily diet pays handsome dividends in protection.

It's easy to determine the correct amount of bran necessary to restore the roughage to the diet of each person. The simplest way is to start with a small amount each day and gradually increase it until the desired results are obtained. For the average adult that might mean about two teaspoons three times a day. Some individuals require as much as three *tablespoons* daily while others do well on one *teaspoon* three times a day. Children between five and thirteen should be started on half the minimum ration —that is, half a teaspoon three times a day. Children between three and five need about half a teaspoon *daily* on the average.

There is an almost infallible way to tell when the ideal amount of bran is being consumed. When the bowel movement is large in amount, well-formed, low in odor, and passed without straining once (or twice) a day, the roughage in the diet is just right. For the first week or so there should be an increase in the amount of gas passed and there may also be a feeling of fullness after consuming the bran. Those are two important signs that the extra fiber is doing its job. If there is any difficulty passing the bowel movement, the amount of bran should be *gradually* increased, say at the rate of an extra teaspoon a day. If the movements become loose or too frequent, it's a sign to cut down on the bran.

The next question is: "What's the best way to take the bran?" That requires some explanation. The most desirable form of bran to use is known as "unprocessed miller's bran." It comes in the form of dry flakes that are easily adapted to anyone's daily diet. Some people prefer to take their bran dry, washing it down with a glass of water or fruit juice. There are, however, dozens of easy and attractive ways to get your daily roughage requirement. For example, you can:

1. Sprinkle it over a dry breakfast cereal with milk.

2. Mix it with cooked cereal, before or after cooking.

3. Add it to your orange juice or other fruit juice.

4. Mix it with yogurt—any flavor.

5. Add it to soups.

6. Mix it with applesauce.

7. Combine it with ground meat to make hamburgers, meat loaf, stuffed peppers, etc.

8. Add it to any home-baked bread or pastry.

9. Include it (as I have done) in any of the sample recipes in Chapter 10.

Within the first seven days you will begin to enjoy the benefits of having restored the essential roughage to your diet. Constipation will vanish almost without exception. Those who suffered from hemorrhoids or other anal/rectal problems may find relief. Victims of diverticulosis—*after obtaining their doctor's consent to adding roughage*—should feel an almost immediate improvement. (You may want to ask your doctor to read "Unprocessed Bran in Treatment of Diverticular Disease of the Colon" in the *British Medical Journal* [1972], Vol. 2, pp. 137–140. If he prefers, he can just drop me a line and I'll send him a copy.) Those with elevated cholesterol levels may want to have their blood cholesterol checked just *before* they use bran to correct their roughage deficiency and then have their doctor repeat the test in six weeks. The results should be gratifying and reassuring for both doctor and patient. (Once again, a good source for your doctor might be "Utilization of Wheat by Adult Man," *American Journal of Clinical Nutrition* 24: 181–193. I'll be happy to send him a copy of that on request.)

Although, as we have seen, no diet in the world is going to reverse the physical changes that are evident in varicose veins, when a person no longer has to strain with each bowel movement, the tremendous pressure that such straining generates is absent and the damaged veins can function much better. At the same time, further vein damage is prevented. Anyone suffering from a severe disease such as kidney disease, diabetes, etc., must have absolute permission from his or her physician before consuming bran.

Another bonus comes in the battle against obesity (see Chapter 8). Bran can be included in nearly every weight-reduction diet—with your doctor's approval, as usual. Being able to eat something three times a day that is chewable, has body, and provides a feeling of fullness—without significant calories—is a dieter's dream come true.

The last benefit of returning to a high-roughage diet

is difficult to explain. It's a kind of indescribable feeling of well-being, the realization that finally, after many years, your body is functioning the way it was designed to function. People who have followed the diet characterize that sensation as "feeling like a machine that's humming along," or "alert and energetic the way I was twenty years ago," or simply, "alive again." When you experience the sensation, you'll understand.

An important question is: "How long should I stay on the high-roughage diet?" The best answer is: "Only as long as you want to feel good." As you notice your appetite for semisynthetic junk food beginning to wane and your appreciation of wholesome food begin to increase, the high-fiber diet will become a way of life. Actually this question answers itself, because after a month on a normal high-fiber diet, there will be no way that you can be convinced to go back to the unappealing low-roughage way of life. Try it and you'll see.

Now let's get down to the specifics of *how* to restore the roughage to our diet. Since not everyone has the same life style, there are three separate high-roughage diet plans. The first one is the "ideal," but since we don't live in an "ideal world," the other two are only slightly less effective:

High-Roughage Diet Plan Number One: "The Ideal"

Avoid: Refined sugar and refined sugar products including sweets, candy, and ice cream as much as possible.

Substitute: Unprocessed honey, unprocessed molasses, sugar-containing fruit (dates, apples, pears, bananas, etc.). Fruit juices instead of soft drinks, home-baked whole-grain pastry made with honey.

NOTE: The reason for avoiding refined sugar is there

is some important evidence that refined sugar alters the dominant type of bacteria present in the colon and increases the possibility of colon and rectal cancer.* It also may contribute to the elevation of blood cholesterol.

Avoid: All refined flour products.

Substitute: Whole-grain-flour products such as whole-wheat bread, whole-wheat crackers, whole-wheat pastries, pies and cakes.

NOTE: Whole-wheat pastry flour is available for home bakers. That makes it possible to prepare everything from cookies to pie crusts with whole-grain flour. Commercial bakery goods made from whole-grain products exist, but are expensive, and may be hard to find.

Avoid: All refined products which are sugar- or honey-coated and presweetened. Rice-based cereals are especially low in fiber, including puffed rice, crisped rice, cream of rice, and the others like them. "Instant" and "quick-cooking" products are also deficient in roughage. That includes instant grits, instant oatmeal, instant rice, instant breading, instant stuffing, and a high proportion of the over one hundred and fifty boxed breakfast cereals.

Substitute: Whole-grain cereal products such as whole wheat, brown rice, whole-grain corn meal (masa), 100 percent rye flour, and carob flour.

Some of the boxed cereals, although they tend to be expensive, are relatively high in fiber. They include the following:

* M. J. Hill *et al.* (1971). "Bacteria and Aetiology of Cancer of the Large Bowel." *Lancet* 1: 95–99; T. L. Cleave *et al.* (1969). *Diabetes, Coronary Thrombosis and the Saccharine Diseases,* 2nd ed. Bristol: John Wright and Sons, Ltd.

1. 100 percent bran cereal
2. Bran flakes (40 percent bran)
3. Bran flakes with raisins
4. Most granola cereals
5. Wheat flakes
6. Puffed wheat
7. Shredded wheat
8. Dry oat cereals without added sweetener

The outstanding disadvantage of some boxed cereals —including the intensively advertised so-called natural products—is that they may contain up to 25 percent (or more) refined sugar. (Even brown sugar is *refined* sugar.) That tends to undercut their value as a source of fiber.

Avoid: All overprocessed fruits and vegetables, including canned, frozen, and other "prepared" versions. (Dried fruit is an exception: It is high in fiber.)

Substitute: Fresh fruits and vegetables eaten with as little peeling, cooking, and processing as possible.

NOTE: As a source of roughage, vegetables are not as effective as whole cereal grains. However, in the "ideal" high-roughage diet they have an important place.

Avoid: "Convenience" snack foods like the new imitation potato chips made from dehydrated potatoes. Also very low in roughage are simulated onion rings, and various pizza-flavored, onion-flavored and cheese-flavored cracker-type chips, crisps, and twists.

Substitute: Tortilla chips if made from whole corn and water, *any kind of nuts*, popcorn, whole-grain pretzels, sunflower seeds, pumpkin seeds, dried fruit, toasted soybeans, toasted wheat, raisins.

NOTE: Most snacks are perfectly suited to a high-roughage diet. If you think about it for a moment, it makes sense. Most traditional snack foods are primitive seeds or grain which humans have been consuming for 50,000 years. Perhaps there is something in the wisdom of the body that constantly drives us back to these high-roughage basic nuts, seeds, and grains.

Special situations: "Ethnic" dishes are an oasis of high-roughage foods in a desert of low-roughage commodities. They have survived the passage of time virtually unchanged and offer an excellent way of adding roughage to the diet in an interesting and appetizing way. A few examples follow:

Armenian: *Bulghour* is high-roughage cracked wheat.
Russian: *Kasha* is buckwheat groats, high in fiber.
Mexican: Authentic *tortillas* are made from high-roughage whole corn ground with lime water. The shells of *tacos, enchiladas,* and *tostadas,* if made faithfully, are of the same ingredients.
Italian: Whole-wheat *pasta* is easily available in Italy; with some searching it can be found here as well. Homemade *pizza* can be prepared with whole-wheat flour.
German: Breading, stuffing, dumplings, and gravy can all be prepared with whole-wheat flour.

Sunday morning favorites like waffles, pancakes, and French toast can make an excellent contribution to the daily roughage quota if they are prepared with whole-grain products.

Baby food is a very special consideration. The majority of commercial baby food can be charitably described as "pap." Generally processed beyond recognition, thickened with generous amounts of cheap low-roughage tapioca flour, they are aimed at Mommy's taste buds, not Baby's nutrition. However, there is an oasis of *relatively* high fiber in the desert of commercial baby food. A list of those highest in roughage follows:

BABY CEREAL

1. Barley
2. High protein
3. Mixed cereal
4. Oatmeal cereal

BABY DINNERS (in jars or cans)

1. Beef noodle dinner
2. Macaroni, tomatoes, meat, and cereal dinner
3. Split peas, vegetables, ham or bacon dinner
4. Vegetables and bacon with cereal dinner
5. Vegetables and beef with cereal dinner
6. Vegetables and chicken with cereal dinner
7. Vegetables and ham with cereal dinner

FRUITS AND VEGETABLES (in jars or cans)

1. Pears
2. Green beans
3. Strained peas
4. Squash

However, as soon as the doctor suggests that the baby is ready for baby food, ask him to approve "real" fruit and vegetables prepared in the family blender. But be sure to get your doctor's approval before adding or subtracting anything from the diet of an infant.

As you can see, Diet Plan Number One requires total commitment to the idea of a natural high-roughage diet. Even with all the fiber it contains, it will probably still be necessary to add about one teaspoon of unprocessed miller's bran to the diet, one to three times a day, to reach the goal of well-formed, low-odor bowel movements passed without straining. (Incidentally, the *relative* lack of odor to the feces results from several factors. On the high-roughage diet there is less decomposition of bile acids, the bacteria in the colon are different, and smaller amounts of refined sugar cut down on putrefaction of the contents of the colon.)

For those who are unable to make the necessary sacrifices—both in time and money—to follow the "ideal" diet plan, there is a reasonable compromise:

High-Roughage Diet Plan Number Two

Basically this consists of following Diet Plan Number One for *seven days*, then switching to Diet Plan Number Three. This approach helps the digestive system to make a rapid transition from the stagnant low-roughage operation to the fast-processing and prompt elimination of a high-roughage diet.

Realistically speaking, there are still many people who will be unable to follow the *ideal* diet even for a week. Because of the cost or the necessity to totally revamp their system of food preparation, they need another way to conquer their roughage deficiency. The best solution for them is:

High-Roughage Diet Plan Number Three

This involves starting right off—today if possible—by supplementing the diet with unprocessed bran in sufficient amounts to insure normal digestion and adequate protection from heart attacks, cancer of the colon and rectum, and the other conditions that result from a low-roughage diet.

Certainly you can improve the efficiency of your diet if you add fresh fruit and vegetables, whole-grain products, and eliminate most of the refined sugar. However, even *if you continue to eat a low-roughage overprocessed typical American diet*, you will obtain *most* of the benefits and *most* of the protection of a high-roughage diet by simply taking your bran three times a day. That makes it ideal for students, working wives, traveling salesmen, men and women in the service, and everyone else who just can't control their daily menu as much as they would like.

In Chapters 9 and 10, there are many sample diets and recipes and useful hints that allow bran to be "smuggled," unnoticed, into the diets of even the most fastidious eaters. Whichever diet plan you choose, from the simplest to the most elaborate, you can be sure that you will eat better, feel better, look better, and—unless five hundred medical experts around the world are wrong—you can look forward to a longer, happier, and healthier life.

8

Obesity— An Avoidable Illness

During the past hundred years a strange and terrible epidemic of a life-threatening disease has spread over our nation. The name of that disease is *obesity,* and it threatens to shorten the lives of over *one hundred million Americans.* Of all the threats to our national health, obesity is probably the most neglected and least understood—and potentially among the most lethal.

According to insurance company calculations,* a person over the age of forty-five who carries as little as *ten extra pounds* decreases his chances of survival by about 8 percent. For every additional pound of excess weight, his risk of dying prematurely rises approximately *1 percent.* The individual who is twenty pounds overweight has a 20 percent greater chance of perishing prematurely, and a man carrying fifty additional pounds has a *56 percent* greater likelihood of an early demise.

Obesity tips the scales of survival against its victims in two ways:

1. Excessive weight makes a person more vulnerable to potentially fatal diseases such as diabetes, heart attacks, high blood pressure and

---

* Statistical bulletins of the Metropolitan Life Insurance Company.

thromboembolism (blood clots that can travel to the lungs with deadly effects).

2. Overweight produces a significantly higher death rate from such conditions as diabetes, inflammation of the kidneys, cirrhosis of the liver, gall bladder conditions, appendicitis, and post-operative complications. In addition, obese people are more likely to develop varicose veins, arthritis, and the various complications of pregnancy. (It may *not* be a coincidence that appendicitis, varicose veins, thromboembolism, phlebitis, and heart attacks have all been associated with our national roughage-deficient diet.)

The worst part about it is that most Americans *hate* to be overweight. They know instinctively that extra fat is unhealthy and unappealing. And they spend billions each year in a desperate battle against extra pounds. They buy costly "dietetic" foods, pay dues at health club and reducing salons, and most expensive of all, seek medical help in losing weight.

The only problem is that up until recently there was very little a doctor could offer a patient who was serious about reducing. The standard approach was usually a pat on the back and the kindly suggestion to "cut down," get more exercise, and avoid sweets. Alternately, the overweight person could visit high-pressure weight-reduction clinics that guaranteed to take off a certain number of pounds for a stiff fee. Both techniques have one thing in common—they rarely produce any *long-term benefit*. Almost anyone can lose weight on almost any kind of diet—but *keeping the weight off* is where virtually every popular diet program fails. The all-too-familiar story is: Adhere to a rigid diet, lose weight, go back to eating "normally," and watch the pounds *relentlessly return*. Over 90 percent of those who lose weight—whether by diet or drugs—gain back every pound, and often more for good measure.

The great irony of our time is that while Americans are begrudging themselves ten calories here and twenty calories there and desperately struggling to limit their carbohydrates to thirty grams a day, millions of others around the world are consuming up to three thousand calories daily and *six hundred grams of carbohydrate* without gaining an ounce! Rural Africans and Asians, for example, remain lean and lithe throughout their lifetimes on high-calorie, high-carbohydrate diets.

Understanding their secret promises to free more than a hundred million citizens from the bondage of obesity and the ever-present threat of the diseases that obesity brings on. As medical researchers pursued their study of the role of roughage in the diet, they made the following observations:

1. Virtually all those in our society who are obese got that way on a *low-roughage* diet featuring refined sugar and ultra-refined white flour products.

2. Many patients complain that although they adhere to the prescribed low-calorie diets, they fail to lose weight, and even continue to gain. (Alibis aside, every experienced physician has observed this.)

3. Throughout the world there are individuals and groups who consume high-calorie diets *without* developing obesity. They include strict vegetarians and rural Asians and Africans.

4. As recently as two hundred years ago in Europe, obesity was rare.

After careful study and analysis of tens of thousands of individual diets, scientists developed the following explanations:

1. Because it is so seductively appetizing (high in refined sugar and ultra-processed flour), the low-roughage diet literally compels overconsumption, making obesity almost *inevitable*. Ice cream, cake mixes, commercial baked goods, canned fruits, soda pop, and commercial dessert products are low in bulk, high in sweetness, and can be eaten in massive quantities. Energetic advertising of these high-profit items also encourages excessive consumption—especially by the least discerning and most vulnerable members of our society, our children.

2. The typical "treatment" of obesity is to place the patient on a *low-calorie* diet. That diet is almost invariably also a *low-roughage* diet. Here are three typical meals on a medically approved reducing diet:

BREAKFAST
½ cup orange juice
1 boiled egg
1 slice toast (from ultra-refined flour)
Tea or coffee

LUNCH
1 frankfurter
1 roll (from ultra-refined flour)
Celery and radishes
Tea or coffee

DINNER
3 ounces of roast beef
1 cup spinach
½ cup carrots
Tea or coffee

That adds up to a grand total of approximately 720 calories, or just about one-third of what the average person needs just to maintain his weight; theoretically it should produce as much as a three-pound-a-week weight loss, week after week. Yet after a token initial loss, many patients are unable to lose weight on this calorie-deficient diet.

The explanation that has evaded doctors for so long may actually be obvious: This type of reducing diet is distressingly deficient in dietary fiber. As confirmation, nearly all patients who suffer on this and similar diets are notably *constipated*. That in itself should have been a clue that the normal operation of the digestive system was being impaired rather than helped.

3. Obesity is rare in *strict* vegetarians, those who consume only fruits, nuts, vegetables, and the like, and who forsake even eggs and milk. Rural Africans and Asians may eat as much as 3,000 calories daily, but since their diets, like the vegetarians' diets, are *high in roughage*, they almost never become overweight.

4. In Europe before 1770 a low-roughage diet was expensive and difficult to obtain—only the wealthy could *afford* to get fat. The poor consumed mostly flour and cereal products—high in *calories* and high in *roughage*—and remained thin.

One of the most-promoted diets in recent history is the so-called low-carbohydrate diet. Untold millions of Americans have tried it in one form or another—with varying results. Although it has been around for many years under many names, the low-carbohydrate diet has always attracted converts because it promises, "You will never be hungry!" In spite of its appeal, that diet has been roundly condemned by medical authorities, including the American Medical Association, as being abnormal and potentially hazardous.

But the basic problem with the low-carbohydrate diet is that it does *half* the right thing for the wrong reason. Based on the observation that the American diet is high in carbohydrates, this popular diet attempts to eliminate most (if not all) carbohydrates from the daily menu. They begin with a goal of "zero" carbohydrates—an impossibility—and then move on to a ration of about one ounce or thirty grams of carbohydrates daily. The promoters of the various diets correctly point out that the average ineffective reducing diet may contain as much as three hundred grams of carbohydrates a day—or more. So, they reason, remove the carbohydrates and the weight must come down.

But they are at a loss to explain why Africans can consume as much as 3,000 calories a day, including *six hundred grams of carbohydrates*, without ever becoming obese. Carbohydrates are obviously not the basic problem—*lack of roughage is*. Once these same Africans adopt our notorious low-fiber diet, they put on weight as much as we do. The story is told of the British medical missionary who recently returned to Africa after being away for many years. When his plane landed at the airport near his former mission, he was amazed and appalled to see, for the first time in his life, groups of *fat* Africans. He investigated further and confirmed that the only basic changes that had occurred in their diet during the past forty years were the addition of refined sugar and ultra-processed white flour. As a matter of fact, the *first* authenticated heart attack in all of East Africa did not occur until 1956—in an African who had adopted a Western diet.

It's only in the past four or five years that medical experts have begun to gain some real understanding of why people become fat. Detailed and sophisticated observations of obese individuals indicate that they have entirely different eating habits from those who have no trouble maintaining their normal weight. Those who tend to become overweight often have a delayed "satisfaction response." That is, they can consume quantities of food before they get the signal from their appetite control center that they aren't hungry any more. Normal eaters, on the other hand, reach the stage of "fullness" much more rapidly— and quickly curtail their intake.

Those who tend to be obese generally consume their food quickly, chew it superficially, and have a taste for items which pack a lot of calories into a small package. In addition, their digestive system seems to operate at peak efficiency, extracting every last calorie from their daily menu. For those people, a high-roughage diet seems ideal. *In effect it counteracts each and every one of these obesity-enhancing mechanisms.* Let's take a look:

1. A high-roughage diet is harder to eat. Instant mashed potatoes and cottony white bread slide down like so much slush. But brown rice, raw carrots, sliced cucumbers, and fresh apples require time and energy to chew and absorb. A person on a high-fiber diet is much more likely to reach the point of satisfaction before he eats too much.

2. A high-roughage diet is much bulkier than a low-roughage diet. By the time an individual does away with a big plate of lettuce or half a bunch of celery, plus a serving of meat loaf laced with miller's bran and a side order of peas, he is hardly in the mood for a heaping bowl of white-flour spaghetti and a couple of slices of white bread.

3. As the items in a high-roughage diet are chewed, large amounts of saliva and gastric juices are produced. This additional liquid mixes with the food in the stomach and causes swelling of the fibers in the food. That distends the stomach and gives prompt and lasting feeling of "fullness"—

that often evasive feeling that so many dieters say they miss.

4.   There is some convincing—although not yet conclusive—evidence that a diet with abundant roughage actually impairs the ability of the small intestine to *absorb* calories. That might mean that someone on a high-roughage diet can actually *eat more and still lose.*

5.   It has been well established that those who consume a high-fiber diet actually excrete more fat in each bowel movement than those on the low-roughage diet.* A dieter on a high-roughage diet can rejoice in the knowledge that he is excreting a portion of his excess body fat as each day on his diet goes by.

6.   The bran portion of the high-fiber diet is a dieter's dream come true. It provides something which he can *eat* and chew three times a day without risking even an ounce of extra weight.

7.   Finally, a high-roughage reducing diet eliminates the bane of nearly every weight reduction program—constipation. *No one on a high-fiber diet is going to be constipated.*

A high-roughage weight reduction diet benefits the dieter in two other ways. It takes off weight, thus reducing the hazard of developing diseases like heart attack, thromboembolism, and all the rest. At the same time, it acts directly on the body to blockade the specific mechanisms that produce these (and other) serious conditions.

---

* A. Antonis (1962). "The Influence of Diet on Fecal Lipids in South African White and Bantu Prisoners." *American Journal of Clinical Nutrition* 11: 142–155.

Most important of all, the high-roughage weight reduction diet is a diet of abundance, not deficiency. Instead of starving your body into abnormally disposing of the accumulated fat, you *eat* yourself into a condition of normal weight distribution. At the same time, you can bypass drugs, shots, pills, and all the risks that go along with them.

All you need to do is follow the High-Roughage Reducing Diet that follows this chapter. Provided you eat nothing but the items listed and you avoid all refined sugar and ultra-processed flour products, you should slowly and *effortlessly* begin to lose weight.

The excess fat will come off gradually—and that's an advantage, for two reasons. First, losing large amounts of body weight too quickly can be dangerous to your health. Secondly, the ideal high-roughage reducing diet is a diet without hunger and without *any deprivation whatsoever*. You can stay on it as long as you want to—preferably for life. Your weight will slowly come down to the ideal level and—as long as you adhere to the diet—stay there. Does it really work? The answer to that is that the diet has been thoroughly tested by hundreds and hundreds of millions of people over the past fifty thousand years. *It is the normal, natural, rational diet of mankind.*

Obesity is a terrible disease—but it is a relatively new disease as far as the history of the human race is concerned. To overcome it, all we have to do is *restore our diets to what they were before obesity existed.*

9

The High-Roughage Reducing Diet

The basic principle of this reducing diet is to normalize the functioning of the digestive system—not to derange it as most other weight-reduction diets do. To ensure your success, there are some important principles to follow:

1. Be certain that you are in good health; a recent physical exam from your doctor is essential.

2. Those who are already suffering from nutritionally oriented diseases such as diabetes, high blood pressure, heart disease, diverticular disease, kidney disease, and others should not undertake *any* diet without their doctor's permission and approval.

3. The High-Roughage Reducing Diet must be followed exactly and precisely. There are no exceptions, no "days off," and no corners to cut. *Addition of excessive fat or ultra-processed starches or refined sugars will result in failure of the diet.*

The basic principle of the diet is simply to cure the fiber deficiency in the so-called modern diet and make normal digestion possible *for the first time in your life.*

Once your body is given the chance to operate the way it was designed to, it will automatically regulate its weight to within the normal range.

When you begin to eat adequate roughage, the following changes should take place:

1. The bacteria in your colon will shift to the lactobacillus-streptococcus forms which encourage *normal* fermentation of the food which you consume, rather than the abnormal fermentation of the low-roughage diet.

2. The amount of fat and fatty acid which you excrete in your bowel movement should increase significantly.

3. The rate of absorption of the food that you consume should decline.

4. The level of lipids ("fat") in your blood should diminish.

There are five things to remember to assure the success of this diet program:

1. *Eat slowly.* The fiber which you consume must have time to absorb the liquid in your diet to provide that essential feeling of fullness and satisfaction.

2. *Don't eat unless you are hungry.* Many overweight people interpret the typical eat-all-you-want diet as a challenge—and one which they rise to meet. Eat as little as you need—and as much as you need—to feel satisfied.

3. *Drink plenty of water.* Fiber needs water in order to make your body work the way it should.

Since you lose about four glasses a day in perspiration, urine, and feces, you need at least eight glasses a day for dieting purposes—and a little more won't hurt.

4. *Don't cheat.* If you really want to lose weight, this diet can help you, but it won't do a thing for you unless you *stay on it.* Sabotaging the diet only sabotages you, your appearance, and your health.

5. *Remember that this is not a "diet" in the usual sense.* You are only getting around to eating —finally—the way you should have been eating all these years. Hundreds of millions of others around the world have lived their entire lives on this kind of diet without suffering any of the illnesses and disabilities that you have come to take for granted. *If they can do it, so can you.*

The menu plan of the High-Roughage Reducing Diet is simple and straightforward:

1. Eliminate all low-roughage foods, all ultra-processed flour products, and all refined sugar.

2. Eat high-roughage foods, including whole-grain cereal products, high-fiber fruits and vegetables, and nuts and seeds whenever possible.

3. Eat moderate amounts of low-fat meat, fish, and poultry. (Incidentally, as you restore the roughage to your diet, you will be amazed to find that you no longer crave large amounts of meat.)

4. Use a moderate amount of fats and oils for cooking and salads.

5. Substitute molasses and honey for refined sugar.

6.   Reduce "hot" spices and relishes to the minimum. There are two reasons for this. First, "hot" spices tend to increase consumption of cereal grain products—from brown rice to hamburger rolls. Second, most relishes such as catsup, steak sauces, pickle relish, etc., are high in refined sugar.

7.   All flour products should be made from one of the following types of flour exclusively:
    whole-grain rye flour
    whole-wheat flour
    soy flour
    whole ground cornmeal
    buckwheat flour (whole grain)
    carob flour.
Bread should contain only these flours without added refined sugar and a minimum of shortening. Other flour products should be made in a similar way. (See the recipes in Chapter 10.) Many of these items can be purchased ready-made in health-food stores—but read the labels carefully to be sure that they contain only these flours and no added refined sugar. (One of the ironies of "modern" merchandising is that we can purchase our daily diet in two kinds of stores: health-food stores and—by implication—"unhealthy" food stores.)

8.   Avoid all "synthetic" products; they are invariably low roughage and will interfere with your diet success. That includes items like nondairy creamer, synthetic whipped topping, artificial sour cream, and imitation *anything*.

9.   Do not eat any of the high-sugar, high-starch items that clutter menus everywhere. They include all "commercial" baked goods, ice cream,

ice milk, imitation ice cream, imitation ice milk, sherbet, "commercial" candy, sugar-containing soft drinks, presweetened cereals, and all other products containing ultra-processed flour, and/or refined sugar.

10. Unfortunately, there is no place for alcoholic beverages on this diet—or on any other medically sound diet, for that matter. Ethyl alcohol, the kind that is in all "alcoholic" beverages, is swiftly converted to sugar in the body. It is a low-roughage (an understatement) food and will undermine the entire diet plan. There is, however, one consolation. Many of those who have followed the high-roughage diet plan find that within a week to a month their desire for alcohol has almost totally disappeared. In any event, there is no way around it—high roughage is "The Thinking Man's Diet," not "The Drinking Man's Diet."

11. Fruits and vegetables should be eaten raw if possible—otherwise, with the absolute minimum amount of cooking and with seeds, skins, and strings as intact as you can manage.

12. An indispensable part of the diet is the addition of unprocessed miller's bran in the average amount of two teaspoonfuls three times a day.

A sample menu looks something like this:

BREAKFAST (2 teaspoons bran with a full glass of water before eating)

Fruit: Raw apple or pear (eaten with the skin) or orange
Cereal: 1 serving all-bran or shredded wheat or

puffed oats plus a small amount of milk and honey

1 egg

Whole-wheat toast (100 percent stone-ground whole wheat)

Tea or coffee (Use honey instead of sugar and a small amount of milk if desired.)

LUNCH   (2 teaspoons bran with a full glass of water before eating)

Roast-beef sandwich consisting of two small slices roast beef on whole-wheat bread (100 percent stone ground)

Lettuce and tomato on sandwich, if desired

Carrot sticks and sliced green pepper

Strawberries for dessert (no sugar or cream—small amount of honey if desired) Use *fresh* strawberries only.

Tea or coffee (Use honey instead of sugar and a small amount of milk if desired.)

DINNER   (2 teaspoons bran with a full glass of water before eating)

Homemade pea soup

Broiled chicken (Fat under the skin may be removed.)

Brown rice

Corn on the cob

Blueberries for dessert (No sugar or cream—use a small amount of milk if desired.) Use fresh blueberries only.

(Only fresh fruits should be used since the canned and frozen varieties *usually* contain additional sugar.)

BEDTIME SNACK

1 cup freshly popped popcorn—no butter or oil, a small amount of salt

You will notice some interesting things about this diet. Generally, no amounts are specified. There are two reasons for that. First, anyone who *really* wants to lose weight will eat as little as necessary to feel "full" so that they can reach their goal. Secondly, within sensible limits, as long as the diet is high in roughage, one cup or two cups of all-bran cereal or an extra helping of meat or brown rice is not going to make that much difference over the long run. Let me emphasize again that this is not a lose-twenty pounds-then-eat-yourself-crazy diet program. *This is a lifetime menu plan designed to restore your body to its normal functioning and* incidentally *to its normal weight.*

An important addition to the diet is two tablespoons of yogurt daily to help convert the intestinal bacteria to the lactobacillus forms which do not tend to split the bile acids nor cause other potentially serious problems.

You can make up your own menu from the following groups of foods. In the process keep these things in mind:

1. The success of your weight-reduction program depends on you. If you cheat, you are cheating yourself.

2. Keep the amounts moderate—sufficient to be fully satisfying but no more than that.

3. Be vigilant to keep refined sugars, low-roughage flours and cereal products, and large amounts of fats from creeping into the diet.

4. Be patient. On this diet you can avoid hunger and the rest of "dieting discomfort"—you don't have to rush. Remember, a weight loss of only half a pound a week adds up to *twenty-six* pounds a year.

Use the following food lists to make up your personal diet plan.

I. MILK PRODUCTS—use in moderation.
Whole milk
Cheese
Skim milk
Yogurt

II. VEGETABLES—any vegetable on this list, in moderation. Prepare any way except fried. Do not add oil or butter except in very small amounts. Cook as little as possible and consume seed, skins, and strings if possible.

Artichokes	Chickpeas or	Rhubarb
Beans—	Garbanzos	Rutabagas
white	Collard greens	Sweet potatoes
pinto	Corn on the cob	Turnips
brown	Black-eyed peas	Oyster plant—
green	Eggplant	salsify
wax	Horseradish	Kelp
red	Kale	Pea soup
black	Kohlrabi	Spinach
lima	Lentils	Winter squash
yellow	Lamb's-quarters	Fried potatoes
Beets	Mustard greens	Turnip greens
Beet greens	Okra	Frozen mixed
Broccoli	Onions	vegetables—
Brussels sprouts	Parsley	carrots
Cabbage	Parsnips	corn
Carrots	Peas	green beans
Cauliflower	Green peppers	lima beans
Chestnuts	Pumpkin	Yams

III. FRUIT—to be eaten raw, with skin *if* possible.

Raw apples	Dried apricots	Cherimoya
Dried apples	Avocados	Citrus fruits

Coconut meat	Cranberries	Loquats
Currants	Elderberries	Olives
Raw figs	Gooseberries	Dried peaches
Guavas	Loganberries	Pears
Kumquats	Raspberries	Dried pears
Berries—	Strawberries	Prunes
Blackberries	Dried litchis	Persimmons
Blueberries	Longans	Raisins
Boysenberries		

IV. ANIMAL PROTEIN—Cook any way *except* fried. Eat moderate amounts.

Beef—carefully trimmed of all visible fat

Veal—carefully trimmed of all visible fat

Organ meats of any species—liver, heart, kidneys, sweetbreads, tripe, tongue. Remove all visible fat.

Pork—lean

Chicken, duck, turkey—remove all fat from under skin *before cooking*.

Fish

Eggs

V. CEREAL, GRAINS AND SEEDS

Bran cereals (without added sweetener)

Buckwheat

Bulghour

Puffed-oat cereal (without added sweetener)

Brown rice

Whole sesame seeds

Hot breakfast cereals made from wheat (except for "quick-cooking" and "instant" forms)

Dried breakfast cereals made from wheat (except those coated with sugar and/or honey)

Shredded wheat (without added sweetener)

Wild rice

VI. BREAD AND FLOURS

Pumpernickel bread (100 percent rye pumpernickel only)
Whole-wheat bread (100 percent stone ground only)
Corn bread (made from whole-grain ground cornmeal)
Rye bread (100 percent rye only)
Tortillas (from whole ground corn only)
100 percent rye flour
Soy flour
Buckwheat flour (whole grain)
100 percent stone-ground whole-wheat flour
Whole-grain ground corn flour
Carob flour

VII. SNACKS—these should be purchased without added sugar, salt, or oil. They are usually labeled "raw," although they may have been roasted.

Peanuts	Pecans	Piñon nuts
Pistachios	Popcorn	Sunflower seeds
Walnuts	Almonds	Beechnuts
Brazil nuts	Cashew nuts	Hazelnuts
Hickory nuts		

VIII. BEVERAGES

Powdered breakfast cocoa (*not* cocoa mixes with sugar added)
Use only honey as a sweetener.
Coffee
Tea

These seven food lists can be combined in the following way:

BREAKFAST (one item from each list indicated) 2 teaspoons of bran with a full glass of water before eating.
III.
IV.
V.
VI.
Coffee or tea or cocoa

LUNCH (one item from each list) 2 teaspoons of bran with a full glass of water before eating.
II.
III.
IV.
VI.
Coffee or tea

DINNER (one item from each list, except two from List II) 2 teaspoons of bran with a full glass of water before eating.
I.
II.
III. (for dessert)
IV.
Coffee or tea

One item from List VII (Snacks) can be saved for bedtime. Remember, eat only *moderate* amounts.

NOTE: Unrefined sweeteners include molasses, honey, and cleaned "raw" sugar. Brown sugar is a *refined* sugar with added molasses and coloring; it should *not* be used.

There is another benefit of the High-Roughage Reducing Diet that deserves comment. Nearly all overeating is motivated at least in part by emotional factors. Tension, anxiety, the excessively fast pace of our daily lives—all encourage overeating. There seems to be something about a high-roughage diet which induces an internal feeling of calmness and tranquillity. After a week or so on the program, that compulsion to rush and to argue and to worry seems to diminish. Most people find it easier to fall asleep at night and they feel more refreshed upon awakening. The tranquilizing effect of the high-roughage diet is only based on individual reports and has not yet been scientifically validated. Make your own observations from your own experience.

Whenever you decide to lose weight, the High-Roughage Diet is there to help you. But you should be aware of one thing—it is habit-forming. After suffering the deprivation and disappointment of previous weight-reduction programs, the pleasure of feeling satisfied, knowing your body is finally functioning as it should—and losing weight in the process—may make it impossible to ever go back to your old low-roughage ways of eating.

10

High-Roughage
Recipes
and
Menu Hints
by
Barbara Reuben, M.S.

The high-roughage recipes and menu hints that follow are the ones that I have developed over the years in my own kitchen. Although bran may appear a little formidable at first —it looks so brown and dry—it really can be a cook's best friend. Each bran flake soaks up moisture like a tiny sponge and if you just give the liquid time to soak in—two or three minutes is fine—the "roughage" becomes "softage" and makes the dish moist and full-bodied.

Cooking with bran has another important advantage—especially these days—since it is an ideal thickener and extender. It's much cheaper than commercial bread crumbs, and it has much more body than flour so it makes meat dishes and canned foods go that much farther.

I've divided this section into two parts. First of all, there's the "quick and easy" section. Sometimes there just isn't enough time to clear off the counter-space and cook a meal from scratch—especially if you have small children. So I've worked out some ideas that will let you change food right off the supermarket shelf into "instant" high roughage. Of course, that's not the ideal way to do it, but getting your roughage that way is certainly better than not getting it at all. Just be sure to mix well and wait a minute or so to let the bran soak up the liquid, and you won't even know it's there!

Canned Goods You can add about a tablespoon of bran per serving with no trouble at all. That supplies half the daily roughage allowance for each person. It also gives the dish a fuller flavor and makes it more satisfying at the same time. Incidentally, I never put too much faith in the number of servings specified on the can label—those canners always seem to come from families of light eaters. Just use your own judgment.

Canned Soups Fairly thick soups like cream of mushroom, cream of celery, cream of turkey, pea soup, bean soup, and chowders seem to take bran the best. I've also found that I can add one and a half cups of water to each cup of condensed soup—instead of the usual one cup—when I use bran. The roughage thickens and extends the final product very nicely. I've never stopped to figure it out exactly, but I have the feeling that the bran I use doesn't really cost anything because it makes so many expensive foods go much farther.

Canned Dinners These preparations are generally about as low in roughage as you can imagine, so added bran is very important. It is a welcome addition to dishes like spaghetti, noodles, lasagne, ravioli, beef stew, hash, chili con carne, goulash, pork and beans, meatballs and all the rest of the one-dish meals that come in cans.

Canned Vegetables You have to use your own judgment here again. The vegetables that come in cream sauces, such as creamed corn, creamed onions, etc., take to bran easily. Most of the others do better if you make the kind of sauce described under "Frozen Foods" below.

Frozen Foods The frozen foods that I've found most receptive to bran are the various frozen vegetables that come with more or less exotic sauces. You can add the usual, almost standard, one tablespoon of bran per person as soon as there is enough liquid melted in the cooking pot to absorb it.

If you serve the kinds of frozen vegetables that don't have their own sauce, you can use this sauce over them:

One tablespoon bran
One tablespoon bread crumbs
Two tablespoons melted butter, margarine, or olive oil
Two tablespoons lemon juice

This is enough sauce for one person, and as usual, it supplies half the roughage requirement for that day.

Dry Mixes. . If you like to use the various "helpers" for tuna, hamburger, and such dishes simply add about ¼ cup of bran to each package. That provides half the daily roughage requirement for each person. Just be sure to use enough liquid to soften the bran—that usually means a bit more than the package instructions specify.

The other kinds of dry mix—the ones you add for making goulash, stroganoff, stew, spaghetti sauce, chili con carne, sloppy joes, Spanish rice, and similar dishes when you're really in a rush—can be enriched with about two ounces of bran to each package.

Seasoned Breadings Those little packets of spices and things that you shake over chops and chicken before you bake them can be made much more healthful if you add up to ⅓ cup of bran to them and mix well before using. When you use your bran this way, you may want to put it in the blender at high speed for a few seconds to make the flakes smaller. You don't need to do it for any of the other types of recipes, but you'll find the breading adheres better if you take the extra time.

Pastry Mixes Cake mixes, pancake and waffle mixes, instant stuffings, and similar products can be supplemented with bran very nicely. Just use the familiar one tablespoon per serving—and bear in mind that bran will be more obvious in some recipes than others. Angel food cake, for example, becomes much more nutritious and less harmful with bran, but it won't be the same angel food cake you have been used to. On the other hand, about 90 percent of the ready-mix flour products will be delightfully enhanced by the addition of bran.

Once you really get started restoring roughage to your family's diet, I think you'll become as excited about it as I am. You'll know that you're giving your loved ones the very best you possibly can and you'll see very quickly that it doesn't make cooking any more difficult. As a matter of fact, sometimes I just measure out the entire bran ration for the whole family first thing in the morning and put it in a small bowl on the kitchen counter. As I go through the day, I supplement various dishes with it until it's all used up. No matter how you do it, after a week or so, I think you'll find that restoring the roughage to your family's daily diet will become second nature.

On those days when you find yourself with plenty of time on your hands—if that ever really happens any more—there are some wonderful recipes made with bran that are really worthwhile. Not only are they tasty and filling, but you'll have the satisfaction of eating the way people used to eat before all that essential roughage was taken away from them. There's just one little detail to remember: Sometimes for one reason or another, a member of your family may not get enough of his or her daily roughage requirement this way. If that happens, simply supplement it with extra bran until he or she has the desired results as described in Chapter 7.

Eleven Main Dishes

Stuffed Pork Chops

6 pork chops cut 1½ to 2 inches thick

Stuffing:
½ cup butter
¼ cup minced onions
1 tablespoon minced parsley

½ cup bread crumbs
¾ cup bran
¼ teaspoon black pepper
½ teaspoon sage
½ teaspoon thyme
2 tablespoons lemon juice
Salt to taste

DAILY REQUIREMENT FOR 6.
SERVES 6.

"Butterfly" each pork chop to make a pocket. Fill the chop with a stuffing made as follows: Melt butter in a skillet. Sauté onions until transparent. Add parsley and bread crumbs and sauté a bit more. Remove from fire. Add the remaining ingredients. Mix well. Fill each pork chop with 3 to 4 tablespoons of the mixture. Brown the chops in a skillet in 2 tablespoons of butter. Cover and let them cook slowly for 20 minutes. Serve with baked apple and brown rice.

Baked Stuffed Fish

Stuffing:
½ cup chopped onion
½ cup mushrooms, cut up
½ cup chopped celery
1 cup (2 sticks) butter
1 cup bran
2 cups bread crumbs

2 teaspoons parsley
½ teaspoon rosemary, tarragon, or marjoram
Salt and pepper to taste
4 tablespoons lemon juice

5- to 7-pound fish

DAILY REQUIREMENT FOR 8.
SERVES 8.

Sauté onions, mushrooms, and celery in butter until onions become transparent. Put bran and bread crumbs in a mixing bowl. Add onion mixture, herbs, and lemon juice to bread-crumb mixture.

Wash the fish inside and out with cold water. Dry well, and rub the inside of the fish with a little salt. Spoon in the stuffing, packing lightly. Skewer or sew opening closed. Place fish in greased shallow oven-proof pan or place on greased aluminum foil in a shallow roasting pan. Brush the top of the fish with oil or lemon butter or cover with bacon strips or slices of salt pork. Bake at 350° for about 50 minutes or until the fish flakes easily with a fork. If you brush with a lemon butter mixture, baste with it occasionally. Suitable for red snapper, lake trout, bluefish, bass, shad, pike, carp, haddock, whitefish.

Variation Use fish fillets and put the stuffing between two fillets or roll the fillets with stuffing. Brush with oil or lemon butter and bake same as above for 30 to 35 minutes or until the fish flakes easily with a fork.

Beef Stroganoff

1 tablespoon flour	3 tablespoons butter
2 tablespoons butter	3 tablespoons minced
2 cups beef stock	onion
½ pint sour cream	½ pound mushrooms,
2 tablespoons tomato	sliced
juice or sauce	1 pound beef tenderloin,
Pinch of nutmeg	cut into strips
1 cup bran	Salt and pepper to taste

DAILY REQUIREMENT FOR 8.
SERVES 8.

In a saucepan over gentle heat blend the flour with 2 tablespoons of butter until the mixture bubbles and is smooth. Stir in 2 cups of beef stock and cook until the mixture thickens. Add the sour cream and the tomato juice or sauce, stirring constantly. Add nutmeg and bran. Add a little milk to reduce the thickness of the sauce.

In a frying pan melt 3 tablespoons of butter and fry the onion, mushrooms, and strips of beef sprinkled with black pepper. Cook about 5 minutes, turning so that the meat browns on all sides. Pour the meat mixture into the sauce and simmer gently for 15 minutes. DO NOT BOIL. Serve with brown rice or flat egg noodles.

Easy Pizza Dough with Bran

Use a biscuit mix and follow the recipe for pizza dough. Add 1 cup of bran to the dough and a little more of the liquid to make the dough soft. Make 2 pies. (If the pies are cut into eighths, 2 pieces equals the daily requirement of bran.)

Meat Sauce for Pizza with Bran

Mix 1 pound of ground meat with 1 egg and 1 cup of bran and a little tomato juice to moisten the meat. Spread on top of the pizza dough with cut-up tomatoes and grated cheese. Sprinkle top with Parmesan cheese. Bake at 400° for 25 to 30 minutes. (If the pies are cut into eighths, 2 pieces of meat sauce with bran contains the daily requirement.)

Macaroni and Cheese

2½ cups cooked maca-
  roni, preferably whole-
  wheat macaroni
3 cups muenster or
  Cheddar cheese

4 tablespoons minced
  onions
1 cup bran
2 cups thin white sauce

DAILY REQUIREMENT FOR 8.
SERVES 8.

Butter a 2-quart casserole. Put half of macaroni in casserole with half of the cheese and half of the onions and bran. Add remaining macaroni and top with the remaining cheese and onions and bran. Pour over the thin white sauce. Dot with butter. Bake at 375° about 30 minutes or until lightly browned.

Thin White Sauce

2 tablespoons butter
1 tablespoon flour
2 cups milk

Dash of salt
⅛ teaspoon pepper

Melt butter. Blend in flour. Cook over low heat until smooth and bubbly. Remove from heat. Add milk. Return to the stove and heat to boiling, stirring constantly. Boil 1 minute. Remove from heat and add salt and pepper.

Beef Stew

2 large onions, chopped
¼ cup butter or oil
2 pounds cubed beef
6 to 8 cups beef broth

3 medium potatoes, pared
  and cubed
4 large carrots, peeled
  and quartered
1 cup fresh green beans
1 cup bran

DAILY REQUIREMENT FOR 8.
SERVES 8.

Sauté onions in butter. Add meat and brown on all sides. Add enough broth to cover. Cover the pan and simmer 1½ to 2 hours. Add potatoes, carrots, beans, and bran. Add more liquid to cover if necessary. Simmer another half an hour.

Meat Loaf

1½ pounds ground beef (or 1 pound ground beef, ¼ pound ground veal, ¼ pound ground pork)
1 cup fine bread crumbs
¾ cup bran
1 egg
2 cloves garlic, minced, or 1 teaspoon powdered garlic (or more to taste)

1 tablespoon Worcestershire sauce
1 tablespoon dry mustard
½ teaspoon sage
½ teaspoon thyme
Salt and pepper to taste
1 cup milk plus

DAILY REQUIREMENT FOR 6.
SERVES 6.

Mix above ingredients together well, moistening with as much milk as is necessary for a soft mixture. Put the mixture into a 9 x 5 x 3 ungreased loaf pan, dot with butter, and bake at 350° for 1¼ to 1½ hours.

Variation: Italian-Style Meat Loaf Leave out milk, Worcestershire sauce, mustard, sage, and thyme. Instead, add 1 tablespoon oregano, ½ teaspoon fennel seed, ¼ cup grated Parmesan cheese, 1 1-pound can of whole canned tomatoes, and enough liquid to moisten well. Pour the rest of the liquid over top of loaf, sprinkle with Parmesan cheese, and dot with butter. Bake same as above.

Hamburgers

2 pounds ground meat   ¼ cup minced onions
2 eggs   Salt and pepper to taste
¾ cup bran

DAILY REQUIREMENT FOR 6.
SERVES 6.

Mix ingredients together well. Moisten with a little milk if necessary. Make into 6 hamburgers. Broil.

Variations:
Meatballs Use above recipe, but make into small balls and fry in oil or butter.

Oriental hamburgers or meatballs Add 2 tablespoons soy sauce, 1 teaspoon powdered ginger, 1 tablespoon sherry, 1 teaspoon powdered garlic.

Italian Add ½ tablespoon oregano, ¼ teaspoon fennel seed, 2 tablespoons Parmesan cheese, and moisten with a little tomato juice or sauce.

Quick Spaghetti Sauce

¼ cup olive oil
2 medium onions, finely chopped
1 pound of ground beef
1 can (1 pound, 12 ounces) whole tomatoes, undrained (sieved or blended)
1 can (8-ounce size) tomato sauce
1 cup bran

¼ cup Parmesan cheese
1 bay leaf
1 tablespoon dried basil leaves or 1 tablespoon oregano
½ teaspoon fennel seed
½ teaspoon black pepper
Fresh or powdered garlic to taste
¼ cup red wine or 2 tablespoons lemon juice

DAILY REQUIREMENT FOR 8.
SERVES 8.

Sauté onions until slightly browned; add ground beef and brown. Add tomatoes, tomato sauce, bran, cheese, and spices. Add ¼ cup Italian wine or 2 tablespoons of lemon juice. Simmer 15 minutes. Serve over spaghetti.

Stuffed Squash

1 large summer squash (12 to 14 inches long) or 2 medium-sized squash
1 pound ground beef
2 small onions, finely chopped
1 cup bran
6 to 8 whole canned tomatoes, drained (1-pound-12-ounce can)
1 egg

¼ cup Parmesan cheese
Fresh or powdered garlic to taste
½ teaspoon black pepper
½ tablespoon dried oregano leaves
½ teaspoon crushed fennel seed
Juice from the 1-pound-12-ounce can of tomatoes
Butter

DAILY REQUIREMENT FOR 8.
SERVES 8.

Cut the squash lengthwise and remove the seeds. (Do *not* peel the squash.) In a bowl mix together well the meat, onions, bran, tomatoes, egg, cheese, and spices moistened with 8 to 10 tablespoons of the tomato juice from the canned tomatoes. Fill the squash and mound up the meat mixture. Place in a roasting pan with the remaining tomato juice and enough water to bring the liquid up to about an inch from the bottom. Sprinkle the tops with extra Parmesan cheese and dot in several places with butter. Bake at 375° for about 1 hour or until squash is tender.

Chili con Carne

1 medium onion, chopped
2 tablespoons oil or bacon fat
1 pound ground beef
1 teaspoon powdered garlic or 4 cloves fresh garlic, crushed
2 cups cooked or canned kidney beans or chili beans
2 cups cooked or canned whole tomatoes
¾ cup bran
1 tablespoon chili powder or ground chili
½ teaspoon oregano
½ teaspoon cumin
Salt and pepper to taste

DAILY REQUIREMENT FOR 6.
SERVES 6.

Fry onions in oil or bacon fat for about 1 minute. Add meat and garlic and fry, stirring constantly, about 3 minutes. Add beans, tomatoes, bran, and remaining spices. Cover and simmer 20 minutes.

Variation Put bean-meat mixture into a 1-to-1½-quart casserole dish and top with corn-bread batter. Bake at 400° for 30 minutes.

Corn-Bread Batter

In a bowl mix:

1 cup stone-ground corn-meal	1 egg
½ teaspoon baking soda	1 cup milk or buttermilk
1 tablespoon shortening, melted	

Beat well and spoon over casserole.

Quick Breads

Drop Biscuits

2 cups flour (preferably stone-ground whole-wheat flour)	4 tablespoons butter
2 teaspoons baking powder	2 cups milk
½ teaspoon salt	1½ cups bran

3 DAYS' DAILY REQUIREMENT FOR 4 PEOPLE.

Sift flour, baking powder, and salt together. Blend the butter into the flour mixture until the mixture looks like coarse meal. (You can blend with a pastry cutter or with 2 knives, cutting the butter into pea-sized pieces.) Add milk and bran alternately, stirring it in little by little. Drop by spoonfuls onto a greased cookie sheet. Bake at 450° for 12 to 15 minutes.

Variation: Cheese Biscuits Add ½ cup grated cheese before adding the milk.

Bran Muffins

1 cup flour (preferably 100% stone-ground whole-wheat flour)
1 teaspoon baking soda
1½ cups bran
½ cup raisins

1 egg, well-beaten
½ cup molasses or honey
¾ cup milk
2 tablespoons soft butter or shortening

3 DAYS' DAILY REQUIREMENT FOR 4 PEOPLE.

Put together dry ingredients and raisins and moisten with egg and molasses or honey, milk, and shortening. Stir only enough to blend. Bake in well-greased muffin tins at 400° for 20 to 30 minutes.

Dumplings

For beef or chicken stews or hearty vegetable and meat soups.

1½ cups flour (preferably whole-wheat stone-ground flour)
½ cup bran
¼ teaspoon salt

2 teaspoons minced parsley
1 teaspoon grated onion
1¾ cups plus 2 teaspoons milk

DAILY REQUIREMENT FOR 4.
SERVES 4.

Mix all ingredients well. Drop from a teaspoon into stew. Cover and let simmer 15 minutes.

Breading

For fried chicken, veal cutlets, shrimp, pork chops, etc. Use half bran and half bread crumbs or half bran and half whole-wheat flour. If desired, bran may be processed quickly in blender, *for this recipe only*.

Banana Nut Bread

½ cup butter
¾ cup honey
2 eggs
2¼ cups flour (preferably whole-wheat pastry flour)
1 cup bran
2 teaspoons baking powder

½ cup milk with 1 tablespoon vinegar and ¼ teaspoon baking soda added
1 cup mashed bananas (2 to 3 large ones)
½ teaspoon vanilla
1 cup chopped pecans (optional)

DAILY REQUIREMENT FOR 1 PERSON IS 4½ SLICES ¼ INCH THICK.

Cream butter and honey. Add eggs. Beat well after each addition. Mix flour, bran, and baking powder together. Add flour to butter mixture alternately with milk mixture. Add mashed bananas, vanilla, and nuts (if desired). Bake in a 9-by-5-by-3-inch loaf pan, well-greased and bottom lined with waxed paper, for 1 hour and 40 minutes at 325°.

Pancakes

Blend in a blender or beat the following:
3 eggs
2 cups milk
½ teaspoon vanilla

1 cup whole-wheat pastry flour
1½ teaspoons honey
1 cup bran

DAILY REQUIREMENT FOR 8.

Blend at high speed or beat. Add more milk as needed to bring to heavy cream consistency. Butter skillet or griddle. Makes thin, light pancakes. Can be filled with sour cream or berries and topped with a bit of honey or sprinkled with raw natural sugar.

Waffles

In a blender put the following:

2 eggs
2 cups milk
1½ cups whole-wheat
    pastry flour
1 cup bran

¼ cup salad oil or
    melted butter
2 teaspoons baking pow-
    der
1 tablespoon honey

DAILY REQUIREMENT IS 2 WAFFLE SECTIONS
PER PERSON.

Blend at high speed or beat well. Add more milk to thin, if necessary, to the consistency of heavy cream.

A rectangular waffle iron with four waffle sections makes waffles four times or 16 individual waffle sections.

Hi-Fiber Crackers

1 cup bran
1¼ cups gluten flour
¼ cup stone-ground
    whole-wheat flour

½ cup sesame seeds
1 cup water
½ teaspoon baking soda
1 teaspoon salt

5 CRACKERS ARE DAILY REQUIREMENT FOR 1,
3 GRAMS ROUGHAGE PER CRACKER.

Put all the ingredients into a mixing bowl and mix well. A soft dough will form. Lightly flour a board or countertop and roll the dough out until it is ⅛ inch thick. Score the dough with a knife into 2-by-4-inch rectangles. Place on a well-greased baking sheet. Bake in a preheated oven at 350° for 10 minutes. Then lower the temperature to 300° and leave another 10 minutes or so until the dough is crisp like a cracker. Makes 40 crackers.

For onion flavor—Add 2 tablespoons of dried minced onion to above.

For garlic flavor—Add 2 tablespoons of powdered garlic.

For cheese flavor—Add 2 tablespoons of grated Parmesan or Romano cheese.

Bread Stuffing

2 medium onions, finely chopped
2 cups celery chopped, stalks and leaves
1 cup butter
8 cups small bread cubes (preferably whole-wheat bread)

1½ cups bran
2½ teaspoons sage
1½ teaspoons thyme
1 teaspoon pepper
Salt to taste

DAILY REQUIREMENT FOR 12 PEOPLE.

Fry onions and celery in 1 cup butter until tender. In a large bowl combine the onions and celery mixture, the small bread cubes, the bran, and the spices. Makes enough for a 10-to-12-pound turkey.

Use the above stuffing recipe with the following changes for a variety of stuffings—all containing bran.

Corn-bread stuffing—Bread cubes should be half corn bread, half regular bread.

Mushroom stuffing—Add ½ cup mushrooms sautéed with onions to every cup of bread cubes. Reduce bread cubes to 6 cups. For recipe above, 3 cups of mushrooms are needed.

Sausage stuffing—Add 1 pound of sausage meat crumbled and browned.

Giblet stuffing—Simmer the heart, the gizzard, and the neck from the chicken or turkey in broth with a dash of pepper, thyme, sage, and salt to taste for about an hour. Add the liver during the last 10 minutes. Chop these ingredients (except the neck) and add to the above ingredients.

Pecan stuffing—Reduce the bread cubes to 6 cups and add 2 cups of chopped pecans.

Chestnut stuffing—Reduce the bread cubes to 6 cups. Leave out the celery. Reduce the amount of onion to 1 small onion, sautéed in ½ cup butter with 1 tablespoon of chopped parsley. Leave out the sage and thyme. Add pepper and salt to taste, and 1 cup cooked or canned chestnuts.

Yeast Bread Dough
(for rolls or loaves)

1½ cups milk
¼ pound (1 stick) butter
or ½ cup shortening
½ cup honey
2 eggs

2 packages active dry
yeast *
4 to 6 cups of stone-
ground whole-wheat
flour
2 cups gluten flour
2 cups bran

DAILY REQUIREMENT FOR 1 PERSON IS
4½ SLICES OF BREAD ¼ INCH THICK.

Scald milk. Add butter and honey and let cool. In a mixing bowl put 2 eggs and the cooled milk mixture. Add 2 cups of whole-wheat flour and start to beat. Add the yeast dissolved in water and 2 cups of gluten flour. Beat. Add 2 cups bran and beat again. When the dough becomes too stiff to beat with regular beaters (if your machine has a dough hook, you can do the entire operation in the mixing bowl), turn it out onto a floured breadboard or countertop and start to knead. Knead in as much of the rest of the whole-wheat flour as you need to have a moderately soft, unsticky dough. To hand-knead the bread takes about 20 minutes. (With the dough hook, it only takes about 5 to 7 minutes.) Place kneaded dough in a large, well-oiled bowl or pan covered with a towel and left in a warm place. Let rise until double in bulk—about 1½ to 2 hours. Punch down. Make into 2 loaves and place in well-oiled loaf pans. Cover and let rise again in a warm place for about an hour—until almost doubled. Dough will rise up over the pan. Place in a preheated oven set at 350° for 40 minutes.

* Into ¼ cup warm water (105 to 115°F) put 2 packages of yeast with a dash of sugar. Let stand five to ten minutes.

Turn loaves out of pan and let cool on their sides. Each loaf contains 1 cup of bran.

If rolls are desired, place balls of dough about 1 inch apart in well-greased pie plates or shallow cake pans—or put 3 small balls in each well-greased muffin tin. Let rise about an hour. Bake in preheated 425° oven for 10 minutes.

Five Delicious Desserts

Hi-Roughage Rice Pudding

¼ cup uncooked brown rice	½ cup honey
	¾ cup bran
4 cups milk	1 teaspoon vanilla
1 tablespoon cinnamon	½ cup raisins

DAILY REQUIREMENT FOR 6.
SERVES 6.

In an 8-by-8-inch baking pan or Pyrex mix all of the above ingredients. Bake at 275° to 300° for 3 hours. Stir a few times during the first hour.

Variation—Use cracked wheat or buckwheat groats (kasha) instead of rice.

Apple Brown Betty

2 cups bread crumbs	1 teaspoon cinnamon or ¼ teaspoon nutmeg
¾ cup bran	
⅓ cup melted butter	Grated rind of ½ lemon
6 cups cored, peeled, and sliced apples (7 to 8 medium)	Juice of 1 lemon
	¼ cup water
½ cup honey	

DAILY REQUIREMENT FOR 6.
SERVES 6.

Mix together bread crumbs, bran, and butter. In another bowl mix well: apples, honey, cinnamon, grated lemon rind, and half of the lemon juice. In a 6-to-8-cup buttered casserole dish put a layer of ⅓ of the bread-crumb mixture, then a layer of half the apple mixture, another layer of the bread-crumb mixture, the remaining apple mixture, and top with remaining bread-crumb mixture. Pour the remaining lemon juice mixed with water over the top. Dot with butter. Bake covered in a preheated oven at 350° for 20 minutes. Then uncover for remaining 15 minutes. Serve hot or cold with whipped cream.

Chocolate Chip Cookies

1 cup butter
1 cup honey
1 teaspoon vanilla
2 eggs
2¼ cups whole-wheat pastry flour

1 cup bran
1 teaspoon baking soda
¼ cup water
12-ounce package chocolate bits

9½ COOKIES CONTAIN THE DAILY REQUIREMENT.

Cream butter; add the honey and beat. Add the vanilla and eggs and beat well. Mix the flour, bran, and baking soda together and add this mixture alternately with water. Beat well after each addition. Add the chocolate bits. Mix the bits into batter well. Drop by spoonfuls onto a greased baking sheet. Bake at 375° for 7 to 8 minutes. Makes 75 1½-inch cookies.

Date-Nut Torte

3 eggs, separated
16 dates, pitted and
   chopped
½ cup chopped pecans
¼ cup honey

2 tablespoons whole-
   wheat pastry flour
½ cup bran
1 teaspoon baking
   powder

DAILY REQUIREMENT FOR 4.
SERVES 4.

Beat the egg yolks. Add the dates, nuts, honey, flour,
bran, and baking powder. In a separate bowl beat
egg whites until stiff. Fold the egg whites into the date
mixture. Pour into a greased 8-inch pie plate and bake
at 350° for 20 minutes.

Brownies

¾ cup flour (whole-wheat
   pastry flour)
½ teaspoon baking
   powder
½ cup butter
2 squares unsweetened
   baking chocolate

3 eggs
¾ cup honey
1 teaspoon vanilla
½ cup bran

4 SQUARES EQUAL THE DAILY REQUIREMENT
FOR 1 PERSON.

Measure flour and mix in baking powder. In a small
pan or double boiler melt ½ cup butter with chocolate. Put eggs into a mixing bowl and beat until light
and fluffy. Add honey and beat well again. Add choco-
late-butter mixture, beating continuously. Add vanilla.
Add flour mixture and bran slowly, beating slowly.
Beat only enough to blend. Pour into greased 8-inch

square pan. Bake at 350° for 15 to 20 minutes. *Do not overbake.* Cut into 2-inch-square pieces, this recipe makes a total of 16 pieces.

Variation—Add ¾ cup chopped walnuts or pecans.

As you continue to use bran and high-roughage cereals in your daily menu planning, I'm sure you will develop some of your own exciting and delicious ways to restore roughage to your family's diet. I would certainly be happy to hear about your experiences, with the understanding that I may use them without obligation in future recipes and menu plans so that families all over the world may benefit. Please write to me at this address:

Barbara Reuben, M.S.
c/o Random House
201 East 50th St.
New York, N.Y. 10022

Appendix

The Case Against Roughage

In my studies of the role played by roughage in the human diet I have tried to be as discerning as possible. I have searched out over six hundred scientific references directly related to the role of roughage in health and disease. In the process I have been alert to any criticisms I could find directed at the safety and effectiveness of restoring roughage to human nutrition.

Let me first report that I have been unable to find any qualified researcher who questions the *safety* of restoring roughage to the diet. Since men and women have been consuming roughage for over 50,000 years, it is inconceivable that any harm could come from *normalizing* the diet of healthy individuals.

I have come across an article in a British medical journal which does criticize some aspects of the role of roughage in our diet. It is entitled "Changes in the Fiber Content of the British Diet," and it is by Jean Robertson. It was published in *Nature*, Vol. 238 (August 4, 1972).

Miss Robertson is apparently an employee of the Fisheries and Food Division of the British Department of Agriculture. Her contention is that the roughage content of the British diet has *not* decreased in the past hundred years or so. She quotes from many tables which assert that the amount of "crude fiber" consumed by Britons has not changed appreciably.

After studying her figures at length, I realized that she had gone astray on the somewhat confusing terminology used by technical experts to describe the fiber in vegetable products. She repeatedly refers to the roughage in food as "crude fiber," while the only meaningful term, in the nutritional sense, is dietary fiber. The distinction is this:

Crude fiber is whatever is left over after treating any foodstuffs with a strong acid, a powerful alkali, water, alcohol, and ether, in turn. In effect this chemical blitzkrieg destroys everything except some cellulose and a substance called "lignin." The original purpose of this test, known among chemists as the "Weende Method," was to protect farmers against unscrupulous feed merchants. Feed samples were tested this way to make sure that a load of fodder was not adulterated with totally worthless "crude fiber." Using this technique to determine the amount of available *dietary fiber* or roughage in the human diet is a serious scientific mistake for several reasons. First, the "crude fiber" method dramatically underestimates the total amount of useful or dietary fiber. The actual amount of useful fiber in food may be 300 to 400 percent greater.*

Secondly, the amount of "crude fiber" in the diet has nothing to do with the issue, since it is *total dietary fiber* that provides protection against disease.†

The third defect in Miss Robertson's criticism of the role of roughage in the diet is a degree of confusion about the relative effectiveness of the cereal fiber in contrast to fiber contained in fruits and vegetables.

---

* *Composition of Foods,* Agriculture Handbook No. 8, U.S. Department of Agriculture, p. 165: "These values (obtained by Weende procedure) may be too low; values obtained by more recent procedures for fiber in some foods are three to four times higher"

† R. D. Williams *et al.* (1935). "A Biochemical Method for Determining Indigestible Residue (Crude Fiber) in Feces." *Journal of Biological Chemistry* 108: 653–666.

Her study equates cereal fiber with fruit and vegetable fiber: However, available evidence indicates that the roughage obtained from whole grains is far more effective—in every way—than that present in fruits and vegeables.

Before a new scientific concept is finally accepted by every member of the medical community, it must go through a rigid series of examinations. In general, that involves eleven major steps. They are summarized below and the score for the high-roughage diet is indicated.

1. Theoretical soundness: *passed*

2. Safety in animals: *passed*

3. Effectiveness in individual animals: *passed*

4. Effectiveness in matched groups of animals: *passed*

5. Confirmation of effectiveness at the cellular level in animals: *passed*

6. Safety in humans: *passed*

7. Effectiveness in individual humans: *passed*

8. Effectiveness in matched groups of humans: *passed*

9. Confirmation of effectiveness at the cellular level in humans: *passed*

10. Retrospective studies (for example, those who ate high-roughage diets in the past experienced less disease): *passed*

There is one final link in the required chain of

scientific evidence before the role of roughage in the prevention and treatment of disease can be declared "undeniable." That involves confirmation by what is called "prospective" studies. It requires groups of animals and then groups of humans to be maintained on both high- and low-roughage diets for purposes of comparison. Careful records are kept of the incidence of disease throughout their entire lifetimes (in the case of animals) or for a period of about fifty years (in the case of men and women). Then the results are tabulated and published. I'm sure that our *grandchildren* will be fascinated by that information.

Since virtually all the diseases caused by the low-roughage diet take about fifty years to develop—with the exception of appendictis, which can show up in twenty to thirty years—if we wait for the eleventh link in the scientific chain to be added, we run the risk of cancer of the colon and heart attacks, as well as the rest of the legacy of suffering that springs from the low-fiber diet.

It seems far more reasonable—at the very least—to go ahead and spend that two cents a day, consume those few spoonfuls of bran, and enjoy the increased feeling of health and well-being that results. Remember that billions of doses of patent medicines are gulped every day with absolutely *no evidence* that they are of any benefit. Billions of dollars go down the drain each year on worthless laxatives; further billions are wasted on unnecessary tranquilizers. If five hundred medical experts are wrong—and the handful of dissenters are right—over the next thirty years you will be out of pocket about $216.00 for the cost of the bran you consume. If the five hundred medical scientists—and the dozens who join their ranks every week—are right and you don't follow their suggestions to change your diet, you'll save the $216.00. But you'll stand to lose a lot more.

Think about it.

Conversion Tables

To Change Customary Units into Metric Units:

When you know	*Multiply by*	*To find*
inches	2.5	centimeters
feet	30	centimeters
yards	0.9	meters
miles	1.6	kilometers
square inches	6.5	square centimeters
square feet	0.09	square meters
square yards	0.8	square meters
square miles	2.6	square kilometers
acres	0.4	hectares
ounces	28	grams
pounds	0.45	kilograms
fluid ounces	30	milliliters
pints	0.47	liters
quarts	0.95	liters
gallons	3.8	liters
cubic feet	0.03	cubic meters
cubic yards	0.76	cubic meters
degrees Fahrenheit	5/9	degrees Celsius

(after subtracting 32)

To Change Metric Units into Customary Units:

When you know	Multiply by	To find
millimeters	0.04	inches
centimeters	0.4	inches
meters	3.3	feet
meters	1.1	yards
kilometers	0.6	miles
square centimeters	0.16	square inches
square meters	1.2	square yards
square kilometers	0.4	square miles
hectares	2.5	acres
grams	0.035	ounces
kilograms	2.2	pounds
milliliters	0.03	fluid ounces
liters	2.1	pints
liters	1.06	quarts
liters	0.26	gallons
cubic meters	35	cubic feet
cubic meters	1.3	cubic yards
degrees Celsius	9/5	degrees Fahrenheit

(then add 32)

Selected
Bibliography

Adamson, L. F. "Serum Cholesterol Concentrations in Various Ethnic Groups in Hawaii." *Journal of Nutrition* 71:27–36.

Ammon, H. V., and Phillips, S. F. (1972). "Fatty Acids Inhibit Intestinal Water Absorption in Man: Fatty Acid Diarrhea?" *Gastroenterology* 62: 717.

Antar, M. A., Ohlson, M. A., and Hodges, R. E. (1964). "Perspectives in Nutrition. Changes in Retail Market Food Supplies in the United States in the Last Seventy Years in Relation to the Incidence of Coronary Heart Disease with Special Reference to Dietary Carbohydrates and Essential Fatty Acids." *American Journal of Clinical Nutrition* 14: 169–178.

Antia, F. P., and Desai, H. G. (1974). "Letter: Colonic Diverticula and Dietary Fibre." *Lancet* 1(861): 814.

Antonis, A., and Bersohn, I. (1962). "The Influence of Diet on Faecal Lipids in South African White and Bantu Prisoners." *American Journal of Clinical Nutrition* 11: 142–155.

Arfdwidsson, S. (1964). "Pathogenesis of Multiple Diverticula of the Sigmoid Colon in Diverticular Disease." *Acta Chirurgica Scandinavica*, Supplement 342.

Aries, V., and Williams, R. F. O. (1970). "Bacteria and Aetiology of Cancer of Large Bowel." *Lancet* 1: 95–99.

Aries, V., *et al.* (1969). "Bacteria and Aetiology of Large Bowel Cancer." *Gut* 10: 334–335.

Bacon, H. E. (1964). *Cancer of the Colon, Rectum and Anal Canal*. Philadelphia: J. B. Lippincott Co.

Badoe, E. A. (1967). *Ghana Medical Journal* 6: 69.

Barker, T. C., McKenzie, J. C., and Yudkin, J. (1966). *Our Changing Fare*. London: MacGibbon and Kee.

Bennett, C. G., Tokuyama, G. H., and Bruyere, P. T. (1968). "Health of Japanese Americans in Hawaii." *Public Health Report* 78: 753.

Berg, J. (1973). "Epidemiology of Gastrointestinal Cancer." In *Seventh National Cancer Conference Proceedings*. Philadelphia: J. B. Lippincott Co.

Berman, P. M., and Kirsner, J. B. (June 1973). "Diverticular Disease of the Colon—The Possible Role of 'Roughage' in Both Food and Life." *American Journal of Digestive Diseases* 18(6): 506–507.

Bird, P. R. (October 1972). "Sulphur Metabolism and Excretion Studies in Ruminants. IX. Sulphur, Nitrogen, and Energy Utilization by Sheep Fed a Sulphur-Deficient and a Sulphate-Supplemented, Roughage-Based Diet." *Australian Journal of Biological Sciences* 25(5): 1073–1085.

Bowsman, C. (1961). *Surgery and Clinical Pathology in the Tropics*. Edinburgh: Livingstone.

Boyce, F. F. (1951). "Acute Appendicitis in the Aging Negro." *Annals of Surgery* 133: 631–643.

"Bran and Diverticular Disease." (May 13, 1972). *British Medical Journal* 2(810): 408–409.

Brocklehurst, J. C., and Khan, M. Y. (1969). *Gerontologica Clinica* 2: 293.

Bruce-Chwatt, L. J. (October 1972). "Effects of Dietary Fibre." *British Medical Journal* 4(831): 49–50.

Bryant, M. P. (1970). "Normal Flora-Rumen Bacteria." *American Journal of Clinical Nutrition* 23: 1440–1450.

Buch, P., and Dunn, J. E., Jr. (1965). "Cancer Mortality among Japanese Issei and Nisei of California." *Cancer* 22: 656–664.

Buckley, R. M. (1967). "Patterns of Cancer at Ishaka Hospital in Uganda." *East African Medical Journal* 44: 165–168.

Burkitt, D. P. (1971). "Epidemiology of Cancer of the Colon and Rectum." *Cancer* 28: 3–13.

Burkitt, D. P. (1972). "Varicose Veins, Deep Vein Thrombosis, and Haemorrhoids: Epidemiology and Suggested Aetiology." *British Medical Journal* 2: 556–561.

Burkitt, D. P., Walker, A. R., and Painter, N. S. (December 1972). "Effect of Dietary Fibre on Stools and Transit-Times and Its Role in the Causation of Disease." *Lancet* 2(792): 1408–1412.

Burkitt, D. P. (1973). "Some Diseases Characteristic of Modern Western Civilization." *British Medical Journal* 1: 274–278.

Burkitt, D. P., and James, P. A. (1973). "Low-Residue Diets and Hiatus Hernia." *Lancet* 1: 128–130.

Camain, R., and Lambert, D. (1964). "Les Hematosarcomes en Afrique Noire Occidentale et Centrale Francophone." In *The Lymphoreticular Tumours in Africa* (a symposium organized by UICC), pp. 42–53.

Carlson, A. J., and Hoelzel, F. (1949). "Relation of Diet to Diverticulosis of the Colon in Rats." *Gastroenterology* 12: 108–115.

"Cellulose Dietary Bulk and Azoxymethane-Induced Intestinal Cancer." *Journal of the National Cancer Institute* 51(2): 713–715 (August 1973).

Cookson, F. B., Altschul, R., and Fedoroff, S. (1967). "The Effect of Alfalfa Feeding on Serum Cholesterol and in Modifying or Preventing Cholesterol-Induced Atherosclerosis in Rabbits." *Journal of Atherosclerosis Research* 7: 69–81.

Cowgill, G. R., and Anderson, W. E. (1932). "Laxative Effects of Wheat Bran and Washed Bran in Healthy Men. A Comparative Study." *Journal of the American Medical Association* 98: 1866–1875.

Cutler, S. J. (1969). "Trends in Cancers of the Digestive Tract." *Surgery* 65: 740–752.

Davies, J. N. P., Knowelden, J., and Wilson, B. A. (1965). "Incidence Rates of Cancer in Kyandondo County,

Uganda, 1954–60." *Journal of the National Cancer Institute* 35: 789–821.

Debray, C., Hardouin, J. P., Besancon, F., and Raimbault, J. (1961). *Semaine des Hospitaux de Paris* 37: 1743.

"Deep-Vein Thrombosis." (October 23, 1971). *Lancet* 2(730): 923–929.

deGroot, A. P., Luyken, R., and Pikaar, N. A. (1963). "Cholesterol-Lowering Effect of Rolled Oats." (Letter) *Lancet* 2: 303–304.

deMuynck, A., Limbos, P., and Janssens, P. G. (1965). *Annales de la Société Belge de Médecine Tropicale* 45: 111.

Denues, A. R. T., and Muna, W. (1967). "Malignancies at the Hospital of Dr. Albert Schweitzer, Lambarene, Gabon, 1950–65." *International Journal of Cancer* 2: 406–411.

de Wijn, J. F. (1970). *Netherlands Milk and Dairy Journal* 24: 106.

"Dietary Fibre." (January 1973). *Gut* 14(1): 69–81.

"Dietary Fibre and Coronary Heart Disease." (April 1972). *Revue Europeenne d'etudes cliniques et biologiques* 17(4): 345–349.

"Dietary Management of Diverticular Disease." (November 1973). *Journal of the American Dietetic Association* 63(5): 527–530.

Dimock, E. M. (1937). "The Prevention of Constipation." *British Medical Journal* 2: 906–909.

Dimson, S. P. (1970). *Archives of Disease in Childhood* 45: 222.

"Diverticular Disease of the Colon and Constipation and Their Relationship to Our Diet." (May 11, 1972). *Nursing Times* 68(19): 564–565.

"Diverticular Disease of the Colon and Constipation. 3. High Fibre Diet with Added Bran." (May 18, 1972). *Nursing Times* 68(20): 620–621.

"Diverticulosis and Diverticulitis." (May 1972). *Practitioner* 208(247): 669–670.

Dodds, C., Fisher, N., Greenwood, C. T., and Hutchinson,

J. B. (August 1972). "Effects of Dietary Fibre." *British Medical Journal* 3(824): 472–473.

Dohi, K. (1941). "Zur Kenntnis der koexistierenden in der Schleimhaut der wegen Krebs reizierten oder amputierten Magendarmpraparate, mit besonderer Berucksichtigung des prapolyposen Zustandes. Anhang Zwei Falle von Polyposis rect." *Gann* 35: 503–544.

Dolbey, R. V., and Mooro, A. W. (1924). "The Incidence of Cancer in Egypt." *Lancet* 1: 587–590.

Doll, R., Payne, P., and Waterhouse, J., eds. (1966). *Cancer Incidence in Five Continents.* UICC Report. Heidelberg: Springer-Verlag.

Domestic Food Consumption and Expenditure 1961: Annual Report of the National Food Survey Committee, p. 13. H. M. Stationery Office, 1963.

Druckrey, H. (1970). "Production of Colonic Carcinomas by 1,2-dialkylhydrazines and Azoxyalkanes." In *Carcinoma of the Colon and Antecedent Epithelium* (W. J. Burdett, ed.). Springfield, Ill.: Charles C Thomas, pp. 267–279.

Eastwood, M. A., and Girdwood, R. H. (1968). "Lignin: A Bile Salt Sequestrating Agent." *Lancet* 2: 1170–1172.

Eastwood, M. A. (1969). "Dietary Fibre and Serum-Lipids." *Lancet* 2: 1222–1225.

Eastwood, M. A. (1969). "Dietary Fibre and Serum-Mitchell, W. D. (1973). "The Effects of Dietary Supplements of Wheat Bran and Cellulose on Faeces." *Proceedings of the Nutrition Society* 32: 22A.

Edington, G. M. (1956). "Malignant Disease in the Gold Coast." *British Journal of Cancer* 10: 595–608.

Edwards, C. H., Booker, L. K., Rumph, C. H., Wright, W. G., and Ganapathy, S. N. (1971). "Utilization of Wheat by Adult Man; Nitrogen Metabolism, Plasma Amino Acids and Lipids." *American Journal of Clinical Nutrition* 24: 181–193.

"The Effects of Dietary Supplements of Wheat Bran and Cellulose upon Bowel Function." (November 1972). *British Journal of Surgery* 59(11): 910.

Ellis, F. R., and Montegriffo, V. M. E. (1970). "Veganism: Clinical Findings and Investigations." *American Journal of Clinical Nutrition* 23: 249–255.

Eshleman, J. I. (1966). "A Study of the Relative Incidence of Malignant Tumours Seen at Shirati Hospital in Tanzania." *East African Medical Journal* 43: 273–283.

Fahrenbach, M. J., Riccardi, B. A., and Grant, W. C. (1966). "Hypocholesterolemic Activity of Mucilaginous Polysaccharides in White Leghorn Cockerels." *Proceedings of the Society for Experimental Biology and Medicine (New York)* 123: 321–326.

Fisher, H., and Griminger, P. (1967). "Cholesterol-Lowering Effects of Certain Grains and of Oat Fractions in the Chick." *Proceedings of the Society for Experimental Biology and Medicine (New York)* 126: 108–111.

Fleish, A. (1946). *Schweizerische medizinische wochenschrift* 37/38: 889.

Food and Agriculture Organization (1949). *Food Composition Tables for International Use*. FAO Nutritional Studies No. 3, Washington.

Fronville, G. (1931). *Annales de la Société Belge de Médecine Tropicale* 11: 445.

Ganong, W. F. (1965). *Review of Medical Physiology*. Los Altos, Calif.: Lang Medical Physiology.

Gennaro, A. R., *et al.* (1973). "Chemical Carcinogenesis in Transposed Intestinal Segments." *Cancer Research* 33:536–541.

Grace, W. J., Wolf, S. G., and Wolff, H. G. (December 1948). "Influence of Emotions and Feeling States on the Behavior of the Human Colon." *American Journal of Physiology* 155: 439–440.

Grove, E. W., Olmsted, W. H., and Koenig, K. (1929). "The Effect of Diet and Catharsis on the Lower Volatile Fatty Acids in the Stools of Normal Men." *Journal of Biological Chemistry* 85: 127–136.

Gustafsson, B. E., and Norman, A. (1969). "Influence of the Diet on the Turnover of Bile Acids in Germ-Free and Conventional Rats." *British Journal of Nutrition* 23: 429–442.

Haenisch, F. (1912). *Deutsche medizinische Wochenschrift* 2: 1356.

Haenszel, W., and Kurihara, M. (1968). "Studies of Japanese Migrants. I. Mortality from Cancer and Other Diseases among Japanese in the United States." *Journal of the National Cancer Institute* 40: 43–68.

Haenszel, W., and Correa, P. (1971). "Cancer of the Colon and Rectum and Adenomatous Polyps." *Cancer* 28: 14–15.

Halls, J. (1965). "Bowel Content Shift during Normal Defecation." *Proceedings of the Royal Society of Medicine* 58: 859–860.

Hardinge, M. G., and Stare, F. J. (1954). "Nutritional Studies of Vegetarians. II. Dietary and Serum Levels of Cholesterol." *American Journal of Clinical Nutrition* 2: 83–88.

Hardinge, M. G., Chamber, A. C., Crooks, H., and Stare, F. J. (1958). "Nutritional Studies of Vegetarians. III. Dietary Levels of Fiber." *American Journal of Clinical Nutrition* 6: 523–525.

Harvey, R. F., Pomare, E. W., and Heaton, K. W. (June 1973). "Effects of Increased Dietary Fibre on Intestinal Transit." *Lancet* 1(815): 1278–1280.

Heaton, K. W. (1972). *Bile Salts in Health and Disease.* Edinburgh, Scotland: Churchill Livingstone.

Heaton, K. W. (December 1973). "Food Fibre as an Obstacle to Energy Intake." *Lancet* 2(843): 1418–1421.

Heaton, K. W. (March 1974). "Letter: Dietary Fibre and Energy Intake." *Lancet* 1(853): 368–369.

Higginson, J. (1967). "Etiology of Gastrointestinal Cancer in Man." In *Tumors of the Alimentary Tract in Africans.* National Cancer Institute Monograph 25. (A symposium organized by UICC). Bethesda, Md., National Cancer Institute, pp. 191–198.

Hill, M. J., *et al.* (1971). "Bacteria and Aetiology of Cancer of the Large Bowel." *Lancet* 1: 95–99.

Hinton, J. M., Lennard-Jones, J. E., and Young, A. C. (1969). "A New Method for Studying Gut Transit Times Using Radio-Opaque Markers." *Journal of the British Society of Gastroenterology* 10: 842.

Hirayama, T. (1963). "Cancer Epidemiology." *Kosei no Shihyo* 10: 13–31.

Hirayama, T. (1967). "Cancer Statistics." *Chugai Iyaku* 20: 258.

Hoffman, K. (1964). "Studies on the Composition of Fecal Flora during a Long-term Nutrition Experiment with a High-Carbohydrate, High-Fat, and High-Protein Diet." *Zentralblatt für Bakteriologie* 192: 500–508.

Hollingsworth, D. F., and Greaves, J. P. (1967). "Consumption of Carbohydrates in the United Kingdom." *American Journal of Clinical Nutrition* 20: 65–72.

Hoppert, C. A., and Clark, A. J. (1945). "Digestibility and Effect on Laxation of Crude Fiber and Cellulose in Certain Common Foods." *Journal of the American Dietetic Association* 21: 157–160.

Horner, J. L. (May 1958). "Natural History of Diverticulosis of the Colon." *American Journal of Digestive Diseases* 3: 343–350.

Hyams, L., Segi, M., and Archer, M. (1967). "Myocardial Infarction in the Japanese. A Retrospective Study." *American Journal of Cardiology* 20: 549–554.

Irving, D., and Drasar, B. S. (November 1973). "Fibre and Cancer of the Colon." *British Journal of Cancer* 28(5): 462–463.

Jones, C. R. (1958). "The Essentials of the Flour-Milling Process." *Proceedings of the Nutrition Society* 17: 7–15.

Kawahara, H. (1964). "Study of the Prevalence of Cancer in Okayama." *Kosei no Shihyo* 11: 20–30.

Kazama, Y. (1920). "Über Darmcarcinom bei Schistosomiasis Japonica; zugleich eine genetische Beziehung zwischen seiner Entstehung und den Parasiteneiern." *Gann* (Japanese Journal of Cancer Research) 15(3): 159–228.

Keys, A., Anderson, J. T., and Grande, F. (1960). "Diet

Type (Fats Constant) and Blood Lipids in Man." *Journal of Nutrition* 70: 257–266.

Keys, A., Grande, F., and Anderson, J. T. (1961). "Fiber and Pectin in the Diet and Serum Cholesterol Concentration in Man." *Proceedings of the Society for Experimental Biology and Medicine (New York)* 106: 555–558.

Kim, E. H. (1964). "Hiatus Hernia and Diverticulum of the Colon. Their Low Incidence in Korea." *New England Journal of Medicine* 271: 764–768.

Kocour, E. J. (1937). *American Journal of Surgery* 37: 433.

Kodaira, T. (1960). "Colon Multiple Polyposis." *Chokucho-Komon Zasshi* 17:60.

Kohler, R. (1963). "The Incidence of Colonic Diverticulosis in Finland and Sweden." *Acta Chirurgica Scandinavica* 126: 148–155.

Komachi, T., Ozawa, H., Iida, M., Tominaga, S., Shimamoto, T., Chikayama, Y., Watanabe, M., Moriwaki, S., Hirose, N., and Kojima, S. (1966). "Study Report on the Cardiovascular Diseases in Japan." Department of Public Health, Osaka University Medical School.

Kramer, P. (1964). "The Meaning of High and Low Residue Diets." *Gastroenterology* 47: 649–652.

Kritchevsky, D., and Tepper, S. A. (1968). "Experimental Atherosclerosis in Rabbits Fed Cholesterol Free Diets; Influence of Chow Components." *Journal of Atherosclerosis Research* 8: 357–369.

Kyle, J., Adesola, A. O., Tinckler, L. F., and DeBeaux, J. (1967). *Scandinavian Journal of Gastroenterology* 2: 77.

Kyle, J. (1968). *Journal of the Royal College of Surgeons of Edinburgh* 13: 136.

Lacassagne, A., Buu-Hoi, N. P., and Zajdela, F. (1961). "Carcinogenic Activity of Apcholic Acid." *Nature* 190: 1007–1008.

Laqueur, G. L. (1965). "The Induction of Intestinal Neoplasms in Rats with the Glycoside Cycasin and Its

Aglycon." *Virchow's Archiv für Pathologische Anatomie und Physiologie* 340(2): 151–163.

Latto, C., Wilkinson, R. W., and Gilmore, O. J. A. (1973). "Diverticular Disease and Varicose Veins." *Lancet* 1: 1089–1090.

"Laxatives and Dietary Fiber." (November 23, 1973). *Medical Letter on Drugs and Therapeutics* 15(24): 98–100.

"Letter: Bile-Salt Patterns in Nigerians on a High-Fibre Diet." (May 18, 1974). *Lancet* 1(864): 1002.

"Letter: Effect of Bran on Bowel Functions." (December 8, 1973). *British Medical Journal* 4(892): 614.

Linsell, C. A. (1967). "Cancer Incidence in Kenya 1957–64." *British Journal of Cancer* 21: 465–473.

Lubbe, A. M. (1971). "A Comparative Study of Rural and Urban Venda Males: Dietary Evaluation." *South African Medical Journal* 45: 1289–1297.

Luyken, R., Pikaar, N., Polman, H., and Schippers, F. A. (1962). "The Influence of Legumes on the Serum Cholesterol Level." *Voeding* 23: 447–453.

Lynch, J. B., Hassan, A. M., and Omar, A. (1963). "Cancer in the Sudan." *Sudan Medical Journal* 2: 29–37.

Majima, S., Karube, K., Narisawa, T., Nohashi, T., and Machida, T. (1967). "Clinical and Pathological Aspects of Cancer of the Colon in 193 Surgical Cases and Results of Surgical Treatment." *Gan no Rinsho* 998–1004.

Maki, T., Sato, J., and Nagaoka, K. (1966). "Familial Colon Polyposis." *Geka* 48: 3.

Mangold, E. (1934). "The Digestion and Utilisation of Crude Fibre." *Nutrition Abstracts and Reviews* 3: 647–656.

Martinez, I. (1968). "Cancer in Puerto Rico." Report from the Central Cancer Registry, Department of Health, Puerto Rico. Personal communication, 1970.

Mathur, K. S., *et al.* (1959). "Dietary Fat, Serum Cholesterol and Serum Lipid Phosphorus, in Different Socio-

Economic Groups in Uttar Pradesh." *Journal of the Indian Medical Association* 33: 303–309.

Mathur, K. S., Khan, M. A., and Sharma, R. D. (1968). "Hypocholesterolaemic Effect of Bengal Gram: Long Term Study in Man." *British Medical Journal* 1: 30–31.

McBee, R. H. (1970). "Metabolic Contributions of Cecal Flora." *American Journal of Clinical Nutrition* 23: 1514–1518.

McCance, R. A., and Lawrence, R. D. (1929). *The Carbohydrate Content of Food.* Medical Research Council Special Research Series (London), 135.

McCance, R. A., Prior, K. M., and Widdowson, E. M. (1953). "A Radiological Study of the Rate of Passage of Brown and White Bread through the Digestive Tract of Man." *British Journal of Nutrition* 7: 98–104.

Medalie, J. H., Neufeld, H. N., Riss, E., Groen, J. J., Kahn, H. A., and Bachrach, C. A. (1968). "Variations in Prevalence of Ischemic Heart Disease in Defined Segments of the Male Population of Israel." *Israel Journal of Medical Sciences* 4: 775–788.

Mekhjian, H. S., Phillips, S. F., and Hofmann, A. F. (1971). "Colonic Secretion of Water and Electrolytes Induced by Bile Acids: Perfusion Studies in Man." *Journal of Clinical Investigation* 50: 1569–1577.

"Methylcellulose in Diverticular Disease." (December 30, 1972). *British Medical Journal* 4(843): 792.

Milton-Thompson, G. J., and Lewis, B. (1971). "The Breakdown of Dietary Cellulose in Man." *Gut* 12: 853–854.

Ministry of Health and Welfare, Japan (1968). *Vital Statistics of Japan, 1965* (Vol. I).

Moore, J. H. (1967). "The Effect of the Type of Roughage in the Diet on Plasma Cholesterol and Aortic Atherosis in Rabbits." *British Journal of Nutrition* 21: 207–215.

Morson, B. C., and Bussey, H. J. R. (February 1970). "Predisposing Causes of Intestinal Cancer." *Current Problems in Surgery* pp. 1–46.

Mulligan, T. O. (1969). "The Pattern of Malignant Disease

in Hesha, Western Nigeria." *British Journal of Cancer* 24: 1–10.

Nast, A. I. (1967). "Epidemiology of Cancer of the Gastrointestinal Tract in Egyptians." In *Tumors of the Alimentary Tract in Africans*. National Cancer Institute Monograph 25. (A symposium organized by UICC). Bethesda, Md., National Cancer Institute, pp. 1–6.

Nigro, N. D., Bhadrachari, N., and Chomchai, C. "Induction of Intestinal Tumors—Choice of Chemical Carcinogen." *Diseases of the Colon and Rectum* 16. (In press.)

Oettle, A. G. (1964). "Cancer in Africa, Especially in Regions South of the Sahara." *Journal of the National Cancer Institute* 33: 383–439.

Oettle, A. G. (1967). "Primary Neoplasms of the Alimentary Canal in Whites and Bantu of the Transvaal, 1949–53: A Histopathological Series." In *Tumors of the Alimentary Tract in Africans*. National Cancer Institute Monograph 25. (A symposium organized by UICC). Bethesda, Md., National Cancer Institute, pp. 97–110.

Omo-Dare, P., and Thomas, H. O. (1966). *West African Medical Journal* 15: 217.

Osaka Medical Association, Department of Health, Osaka, Center for Adult Diseases, Osaka (1967). *Report of Cancer Registration in Osaka*, No. 9.

Oschner, H. C., and Bargen, J. A. (1935). *Annals of Internal Medicine* 9: 282.

Painter, N. S., Almeida, A. Z., and Colebourne, K. W. (1972). "Unprocessed Bran in Treatment of Diverticular Disease of the Colon." *British Medical Journal* 2: 137–140.

Parks, T. G. (1968). *Proceedings of the Royal Society of Medicine* 61: 932.

Parks, T. G. (1973). *Rendiconti Romani di gastroenterologia* 5: 25.

Parks, T. G. (July 1973). "The Role of Dietary Fibre in

the Prevention and Treatment of Diseases of the Colon."
Proceedings of the Royal Society of Medicine 66(7):
681–683.

Parsons, D. S. (January 1973). "Dietary Fibre, Stool Output, and Transit-Time." *Lancet* 1(795): 152.

Payler, D. K. (June 1973). "Food Fibre and Bowel Behavior." *Lancet* 1(816): 1394.

Platt, B. S. (1962). *Tables of Representative Values of Foods Commonly Used in Tropical Countries.* Medical Research Council Special Research Series No. 302, HMSO, London.

Pomare, E. W., and Heaton, K. W. (November 1973). "Alteration of Bile Salt Metabolism by Dietary Fibre (Bran)." *British Medical Journal* 4(887): 262–264.

Ponka, J. L., and Shaalan, A. K. (July 1964). "Changing Aspects in Surgery of Diverticulitis." *Archives of Surgery* 89: 31–42.

"Possible Relationships between Bowel Cancer and Dietary Habits." (September 1971). *Proceedings of the Royal Society of Medicine* 64(9): 964.

Prates, M. D., and Torres, F. O. (1965). "A Cancer Survey in Lourenco Marques, Portuguese East Africa." *Journal of the National Cancer Institute* 35: 729–757.

Prior, I. A. M. (1971). "The Price of Civilization." *Nutrition Today* 62: 2–11.

"Proceedings: The Effect of Bran on Steaming Patterns in Normal Volunteers and Patients with Colonic Diverticular Disease." (October 1973). *Gut* 14(10): 817.

"Proceedings: The Effect of Bran on Transit Time, Bile Acid Concentration and Motility in Colonic Diverticular Disease." (April 1974). *British Journal of Surgery* 61(4): 323.

Robertson, J. (August 1972). "Changes in the Fibre Content of the British Diet." *Nature* 238(362): 290–292.

Schowengerdt, C. G., *et al.* (1969). "Diverticulosis, Diverticulitis and Diabetes." *Archives of Surgery* 98: 500–504.

Schubert, W. J. (1965). *Lignin Biochemistry.* New York and London: Academic Press.

Scotch, N. A. (1960). "A Preliminary Report on the Relation of Sociocultural Factors to Hypertension among the Zulu." *Annals of the New York Academy of Science* 84: 1000–1009.

Sealock, R. R., Basinski, D. H., and Murlin, J. R. (1941). "Apparent Digestibility of Carbohydrates, Fats, and Indigestible Residue in Whole Wheat and White Breads." *Journal of Nutrition* 22: 589–596.

Seftel, H. C., Kew, M. C., and Bersóhn, I. (1970). "Myocardial Infarction in Johannesburg Bantu." *South African Medical Journal* 44: 8–12.

Segi, M., *et al.* (1965). "Cancer Mortality in Japan (1899–1962)." Department of Public Health, Tohoku University School of Medicine, Sendai, Japan.

Shaper, A. G. (1970). In *Atherosclerosis: Proceedings of the Second International Symposium,* R. J. Jones, ed. Berlin and New York: Springer, p. 314.

Short, A. R. (1946). *The Causation of Appendicitis.* Bristol, England: John Wright & Sons, Ltd.

Shurpalekar, K. S., Doraiswamy, T. R., Saundaravalli, O. E., and Narayana, Rao M. (1971). "Effect of Inclusion of Cellulose in an 'Atherogenic' Diet on the Blood Lipids of Children." *Nature* (London) 232: 554–555.

Sinclair, H. (1971). "Modern Diet and Degenerative Disease." In R. Waller, ed., *Just Consequences.* London, England: Charles Knight & Co., Ltd.

Smith, E. *The Food of the Poorer Labouring Classes in England.* Sixth Report of the Medical Officer of the Privy Council, 1863. Appendix 6 [3416], HC 1864 XXVIII, 216.

Southgate, D. A. T. (1960). "Determination of Carbohydrates in Foods. II. Unavailable Carbohydrates." *Journal of the Science of Food and Agriculture* 20: 331–335.

Spjut, H. J., and Spratt, J. S., Jr. (1965). "Endemic and

Morphological Similarities Existing Between Spontaneous Neoplasms in Man and 3:2'-dimethyl-4-aminodiphenyl Induced Colonic Neoplasms in Rats." *Annals of Surgery* 161: 309–324.

Stanley, M., Paul, D., Gacke, D., and Murphy, J. (1972). "Comparative Effects of Cholestyramine Metamucil and Cellulose on Bile Salt Excretion in Man." *Gastroenterology* 62: 816.

Steiner, P. E. (1954). *Cancer: Race and Geography*. Baltimore: Williams & Wilkins Co.

Stemmermann, G. N. (1970). *Archives of Environmental Health* 20: 266.

Stout, C., Morrow, J., Brandt, E. N., Jr., and Wolf, S. (1964). "Unusually Low Incidence of Death from Myocardial Infarction." *Journal of the American Medical Association* 188: 845–849.

Streicher, M. K., and Quirk, R. M. (1943). "Constipation: Clinical and Roentgenologic Evaluation of the Use of Bran." *American Journal of Digestive Diseases* 10: 179–181.

Thijs, A. (1957). "Considerations sur les tumeurs malignes des indigenes du Congo belge et du Ruanda-Urundi. A propose de 2,536 cas." *Annales de la Société Belge de Médecine Tropicale* 37: 483–514.

Trowell, H. C. (1960). *Non-infective Diseases in Africa*. London, England: Edward Arnold, Ltd.

Trowell, H. (April 1972). "Dietary Fibre and Coronary Heart Disease." *Revue Européenne d'etudes cliniques et biologiques* 17(4): 345–349.

Trowell, H. (1972). "Ischemic Heart Disease and Dietary Fiber." *American Journal of Clinical Nutrition* 15: 926–932.

Trowell, H. C. (1972). "Fiber: A Natural Hypocholesteremic Agent." *American Journal of Clinical Nutrition* 25: 464–465.

Trowell, H. (January 1974). "Letter: Fibre and Obesity." *Lancet* 1(847): 95.

Truswell, A. S., and Mann, J. J. (1972). "Epidemiology

of Serum Lipids in Southern Africa." *Atherosclerosis* 16: 15–29.

Vijayagopalan, P., and Kurup, P. A. (1970). "Effect of Dietary Starches on the Serum, Aorta and Hepatic Lipid Levels in Cholesterol-Fed Rats." *Atherosclerosis* 11: 257–264.

Walker, A. R. P. (1947). "The Effect of Recent Changes of Food Habits on Bowel Motility." *South African Medical Journal* 21: 590–596.

Walker, A. R. P. (1961). "Crude Fibre, Bowel Motility and Pattern of Diet." *South African Medical Journal* 35: 114–115.

Walker, A. R. P. (1964). "Overweight and Hypertension in Emerging Populations (editorial)." *American Heart Journal* 68: 581–585.

Walker, A. R. P. (1971). "Diet, Bowel Motility, Faeces Composition and Colonic Cancer." *South African Medical Journal* 45: 377–379.

Walker, A. R., Richardson, B. D., Walker, B. F., and Woolford, A. (April 1973). "Appendicitis, Fibre Intake and Bowel Behaviour in Ethnic Groups in South Africa." *Postgraduate Medical Journal* 49: 243–249.

Walker, A. R. (May 1974). "Editorial: Dietary Fibre and the Pattern of Disease." *Annals of Internal Medicine* 80(5): 663–664.

Wangensteen, O. H., and Bowers, W. F. (1937). *Archives of Surgery, Chicago,* 34: 496.

Ward, J. M., Yamamoto, R. S., and Brown, C. A. "Pathology of Intestinal Neoplasms and Other Lesions in Rats Exposed to Azoxymethane." *Journal of the National Cancer Institute* 5. (In press.)

Watt, B. K., and Merrill, A. L. (1963). *Composition of Food, Raw, Processed and Prepared.* Agriculture Handbook No. 8, U.S. Department of Agriculture, Washington, D.C.

Wein, E. E., and Wilcox, E. B. (August 1972). "Serum Cholesterol from Pre-adolescence through Young Adulthood." *Journal of the American Dietetic Association* 61 (2): 155–158.

Weisburger, H. H. (1973). "Model Studies on the Etiology of Colon Cancer." In *Topics in Chemical Carcinogenesis* (W. Nakahara *et al.*, eds.). Baltimore, Md.: University Park Press, pp. 159–174.

Weisburger, J. H., and Weisburger, E. K. (1967). "Tests for Chemical Carcinogens." In *Methods in Cancer Research* (Busch, H., ed.), Vol. 1, p. 325. New York: Academic Press.

Weisburger, J. H. (1973). "Chemical Carcinogenesis in the Gastrointestinal Tract." In *Seventh National Cancer Conference Proceedings.* Philadelphia: J. B. Lippincott Co.

Westhuizen, J. van der, Mbizvo, M., and Jones, J. I. (1972). "Letter: Unrefined Carbohydrate and Glucose Tolerance." *Lancet* 2, 719.

Williams, R. D., and Olmsted, W. H. (1935). "A Biochemical Method for Determining Indigestible Residue (Crude Fibre) in Feces, Lignin, Cellulose and Non-Water-Soluble Hemi-celluloses." *Journal of Biological Chemistry* 108: 653–666.

Williams, R. D., and Olmsted, W. H. (1936). "The Effect of Cellulose, Hemicellulose, and Lignin on the Weight of the Stool. A Contribution to the Study of Laxation in Man." *Journal of Nutrition* 11: 433–449.

Winitz, M., *et al.* (1965). "Evaluation of Chemical Diets as Nutrition for Man-in-Space." *Nature* 205: 741–743.

Wittig, V. G., Wildner, G. P., and Ziebarth, D. (1971). "Der Einfluß der Ingesta auf die Kanzerisierung des Rattendarms durch Dimethylhydrazin." *Archiv für Geschwulstforschung* 37: 105–115.

Wozasek, O., and Steigmann, F. (1942). "Studies on Colon Irritation. III. Bulk of Faeces." *American Journal of Digestive Diseases* 9: 423–425.

Wood, T. M. (1970). "Cellulose and Cellulolysis." *World Review of Nutrition and Dietetics* 12: 227–265.

Wynder, E. L., and Shigematsu, T. (1967). "Environ-

The Save Your Life Diet

mental Factors of Cancer of the Colon and Rectum."
Cancer 20: 1520–1561.

Wynder, E. L., Kajitani, T., Ishikawa, S., *et al.* (1969).
"Environmental factors of Cancer of the Colon and
Rectum. II. Japanese Epidemiological Data." *Cancer*
23: 1210–1220.

172

About the Author

DR. DAVID REUBEN received his medical degree at the University of Illinois College of Medicine. He served his internship and residency at Cook County Hospital. After serving as a medical officer in the U.S. Air Force, he entered private practice. Dr. Reuben's books have sold approximately 15 million copies in twenty-five countries and have been translated into twenty-two languages.

BARBARA REUBEN, who provided recipes for this book, received her B.A. from Emerson College and her M.S. from Hofstra University. She is a gourmet cook, speaks five languages, and is responsible for most of her husband's accomplishments.

5 of the best reasons to eat nutritiously.

Ballantine
brings you...
FOOD
for
THOUGHT

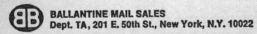